THE NATIVE AMERICANS

1899 mural by Arthur Thomas imagining the 1679 landing of René-Robert Cavelier, sieur de La Salle, at the portage between the St. Joseph and Kankakee rivers.

PEOPLING INDIANA · VOLUME 2

THE NATIVE AMERICANS

ELIZABETH GLENN & STEWART RAFERT

Indiana Historical Society Press | Indianapolis, 2009

Printed in the United States of America

This book is a publication of the
Indiana Historical Society Press
Eugene and Marilyn Glick Indiana History Center
450 West Ohio Street
Indianapolis, Indiana 46202-3269 USA
www.indianahistory.org
Telephone orders 1-800-447-1830
Fax orders 1-317-234-0562
Online orders @ shop.indianahistory.org

Photo credits for front cover: Indiana Historical Society collections

Portions of this book previously appeared in *Peopling Indiana: The Ethnic Experience*, ed.
Robert M. Taylor Jr. and Connie A. McBirney (Indianapolis: Indiana Historical Society, 1996).

The paper in this publication meets the minimum requirements of American National
Standard for Information Sciences—Permanence of Paper for Printed Library Materials,
ANSI Z39. 48–1984

Library of Congress Cataloging-in-Publication Data

Glenn, Elizabeth J.
  The Native Americans / Elizabeth Glenn and Stewart Rafert.
     p. cm. — (Peopling Indiana ; v. 2)
  Includes bibliographical references and index.
  ISBN 978-0-87195-280-6 (alk. paper)
  1. Indians of North America—Indiana—History. 2. Indians of North America—Indiana—
Ethnic identity. 3. Indiana—Ethnic relations. 4. Indiana—History. I. Rafert, Stewart.
II. Title.
  E78.I53G54 2009
  305.8009772—dc22

                                        2009036913

Publication of this book was made possible by the generous support of the
Mississinewa Battlefield Society, Inc.

To the Native Americans of Indiana, past and present.

To Stewart Rafert's ancestors of the German settlement
of Hancock County, Indiana. Their commitment to preservation
of farm land and to education lives on as the seventh
generation continues the heritage.

Contents

Acknowledgments

The authors would like to gratefully acknowledge several people who assisted in writing this book. Donald R. Cochran, director of Archaeological Resources Management Services, Ball State University, retired, vetted the archaeological section. Thomas A. Charles, senior research analyst, Bureau of Business Research, Ball State University, extracted the Indiana Indian population from the last census. Bruce A. Thompson, technical supervisor, Carmel-Clay School system, retired, converted the census data to a rather dated spread sheet and smoothed out numerous computer glitches as they occurred. Angela Hoseth of the History Media Center, University of Delaware, assisted with scanning images.

Elizabeth Glenn
Department of Anthropology, Ball State University

The Indiana Historical Society (IHS) has encouraged and supported my research and writing on American Indians beginning with my doctoral degree in the 1970s. I want to thank Teresa Baer, managing editor, Family History Publications, IHS Press, for encouraging me and co-author Elizabeth Glenn to completely rewrite and greatly expand an earlier essay on the Indians of Indiana published in the Society's book *Peopling Indiana: The Ethnic Experience* (1996, 2009).

My professional career has long been connected with the Indiana Miami people, incorporated as the Miami Nation of Indians of Indiana since 1937. For this volume, I want to thank Vice Chief John Dunnagan, tribal council member Marilyn Rumsey, and Scott Shoemaker, artist and leader of Miami language camps for Miami children. They have answered various questions and have helped keep a Miami voice and presence in this volume.

Stewart Rafert
Department of History, University of Delaware

Introduction

In 1996 the Indiana Historical Society published a volume titled *Peopling Indiana: The Ethnic Experience.*[1] For that volume Elizabeth Glenn and Stewart Rafert cowrote the essay on Native Americans. As the Society expands this project into a volume-by-volume exploration of Indiana's ethnic diversity, the authors were pleased for the opportunity to enlarge an all-too-brief article into a fuller exploration of the history of Indiana's Native American population. The division of labor remained the same—Glenn prepared the up-to-removal segment, and Rafert the post-removal period. If nothing else, it was a joy for the authors to collaborate again as they have several times in the past.

As a volume on Native Americans that constitutes part of a series on ethnic groups in the state of Indiana, some unique properties of the central subject should be clarified at the start. The first is that "Native American" does not identify a single ethnic group but is rather one of the generic terms for the hundreds of distinct ethnic groups found in North America at the time of European colonization. Multiple groups were found initially by Europeans in Indiana. Even more traversed, and some stayed in, the state as people were displaced from particularly the east or north. Each of these groups was distinct in that they had linguistic and cultural differences that gave them separate ethnicities. Thus this volume will discuss several ethnic groups, although unfortunately space will not allow for full exploration of their differences.

Another problem is that not one of these Native American ethnic groups associated with the territory that became Indiana lived entirely within that territory throughout the more than three hundred years of European contact. The Miami and the groups derived from them (the Wea, Piankashaw, and Eel River) were most closely associated with the future Indiana, but not even they were entirely within the area all the time. Groups such as the Potawatomi, Shawnee, and Kickapoo/Mascouten, although found for long periods in the region that would become Indiana, had the majority of their population living elsewhere. Others, such as elements of the Delaware, Nanticoke, and Mahican, were relatively brief sojourners. Still others, such as the Winnebago and Wyandot, were special-purpose residents, non-Indiana natives who may have set up temporary villages in Indiana in order to meet with other Indians for religious or political reasons.

Rather than artificial boundaries based on political rationales, the Native Americans were initially concerned with ecological zones within which they could make a living and, as time passed, with regional events that drew them to or forced them from the area. Thus the more familiar approach to writing about the history and/or culture of Native Americans is a tribe-by-tribe treatment or by broad culture areas based on ecological factors. These approaches do exist for tribes found at one time or another in Indiana. Stewart Rafert and Bert Anson have both written histories of the Miami, and James A. Clifton and R. David Edmunds have done the same for the Potawatomi, with Clifton's book emphasizing culture change through time.[2] The early portions of Arrell M. Gibson's book on the Kickapoo cover their stay in Indiana.[3] A chapter in Clinton A. Weslager's history of the Delaware is devoted to their sojourn in Indiana, and Amy C. Schutt's book on the Delaware gives a more recent interpretation.[4] A work on the Delaware that is devoted entirely to their stay in Indiana is the dissertation by Roger James Ferguson.[5] Probably the most thorough treatment of a culture area that describes all the groups associated with what was to be Indiana is found in the Smithsonian Institution's volume *Northeast*, edited by Bruce Trigger.[6]

Whatever descriptive format is chosen to look at the history of Native Americans, one has to remember that they were preliterate. Thus much of what we know of their culture, including their concerns, strategies, philosophies, interrelationships, and history, we know through the eyes and writings of outside European observers. These observers were not unbiased. Not only did they consider their ethnic groups superior to the Native Americans, but since they were generally explorers, traders, missionaries, soldiers, settlers, or political administrators, they were intent on getting something to their own advantage from the American Indian. If affairs worked to the European recorder's advantage, those particular natives were good, honorable, and handsome people. If a contact did not work out for the European, those natives were brutish, dishonorable, and ugly. Additionally, during the early contact periods only small snapshots of the total picture for an area were actually sought, seen, or recorded by these early observers. One aspect of the scene missing and/or misrepresented throughout the early record was something as basic as a population count for the various groups encountered. Early French records gave most of the groups associated with Indiana maximum population counts numbering in the thousands, not tens of thousands. Not only did the recorders never "see" everyone due to the limitations of the early contacts, consistent undercounting has many times itself served as a form of bias.[7]

Another general aspect of this ethnic narrative should be mentioned relative to the context of volumes on other ethnic groups in the Peopling Indiana Series. Inherent in the stories of other ethnic groups is the underlying theme "We came, we increased, and we prospered," and then "we retained or reintroduced some of our old ethnic practices to remember our heritage." However, the original inhabitants have had a different experience. Even before direct contact between Europeans and Native Americans in this region, epidemics of European diseases traveling traditional trade routes caused a deterioration of the populations of the region. After contact, that deterioration continued and was exacerbated with the addition of warfare, economic depletion, displacement, forced cultural change, and other negative aspects of that contact. Thus the Native American population shrank, their resources were lost, their way of life was threatened, they were demoralized by endless broken promises, and, until very recently, their identity and beliefs were devalued. Thus much of their story is of persistence against great odds using numerous strategies just to survive as a people with some semblance of their cultural identity.

Indiana is not alone in constricting Native American history within a modern state boundary rather than the usual approach of examining the ethnography of a single tribe. Just among the states that were carved out of the Northwest Territory two similar approaches appear. Charles E. Cleland in *Rites of Conquest: The History and Culture of Michigan's Native Americans* and Robert E. Bieder in *Native American Communities in Wisconsin, 1600–1960: A Study of Tradition and Change* have done Native American histories for their more northern states.[8] Attempting a similar feat for Indiana Native American history presents some differences because of the state's more southern location. For the first one hundred years of that history, Indiana's native occupants were players in the French-constructed fur trade, but the endeavors did not have the centrality of Wisconsin and Michigan. There were no major trading or administrative centers in Indiana (as in Michilimackinac, Green Bay, and Detroit) and no major mission sites.

The three main French outposts in Indiana, Forts Miamis, Ouiatenon, and Vincennes, although important to the French for protecting the transit through Indiana, do not provide the volume of information found further north. After the end of the French and English trade period, as the Americans took actual control of the area from 1800 on, the onrush of settlers along the Ohio River was so disruptive for Indiana's Native Americans that continuity of

their way of life was difficult. Military defeat, land loss, rapid population depletion, some acculturation, and removal were accomplished within two generations. These effects were not so dramatic or all encompassing further north. So
this history differs somewhat from the history told, applying the same meth-
odology, about areas further north.

The history of the future Indiana opens with the region as a vacant zone.
During the mid-seventeenth century, the "Crossroads of America" seemed to
be a crossroads for Iroquois war parties, making it a dangerous place to live.
One assumes to call it "vacant" is a bit of an exaggeration, but it is certainly
an era for which information is nonexistent and candidates for the "original"
native population are hard to identify. This is in part because Europeans, ap-
proaching exploration of the Upper Great Lakes from the north, arrived late in
exploring this more southern region and in part because all native ethnicities
later found in this region were first found further north or east.

Contact with the French who followed the Native Americans as they
returned to the future Indiana from the north following decades of intertribal
warfare meant continued participation in the fur trade, exposure to Catholic
mission efforts, becoming part of the discovery/military competition between
European powers for New World dominance, and continued and more intense
exposure to Old World diseases to which New World peoples had limited to
no immunity. In the Indiana area a change in the mid-eighteenth century to
British control changed life little because of the light footprint of the English,
who primarily administered the area from major posts while preexisting trade
networks continued. The exception was the new British policy discouraging
leniency in distributing presents to tribes. It took a native rebellion against the
British, called Pontiac's War, to cause a rethinking on Great Britain's part. This
period of the French and British fur trade, lasting for more than one hundred
years, was marked for the Native Americans by selective culture change as they
chose between various material goods, political objectives, and demographic
changes introduced from outside. It was also marked by the devastating effects
of disease and alcohol, also introduced from outside, and the disruption of
European powers seeking to gain political, economic, and cultural hegemony
in North America. Yet the Upper Great Lakes, including the future Indiana,
were still the domain of the Native Americans through the eighteenth century.

This was to change when the Americans prevailed in their revolution
against Britain. Much to the surprise of the Indians, in 1783 England conceded
the future Northwest Territory to the Americans. Native Americans knew the

stakes had changed because Americans wanted their lands, not their economic cooperation and alliance. Almost immediately the Americans began to acquire bits of lands north of the Ohio River through treaty. They then exerted pressure for U.S. expansion through a series of invasions, both with major armies and search and destroy raids, of the future Ohio and Indiana territories in the early 1790s. As a result of military and other pressures, by 1795 the first lands in what would become Indiana were ceded. Indiana Territory was organized in 1800, and under Governor William Henry Harrison, the southern third of Indiana was ceded between 1803 and 1809, beginning a flood of Euro-American immigration. The result was that in "the Land of Indians," Indians were no longer the majority population by the end of the first decade in 1800. In a generation circumstances had changed dramatically.

The War of 1812 exhausted both the slim military option that existed for the Indian population and its economic stability. After the war Indiana became a state in 1816, and land cession treaties within its boundaries resumed in 1818. These treaties began the process of not only ceding land but also removing the Native American population from Indiana to areas west of the Mississippi River. Thus group by group the Delaware, Piankashaw, Kickapoo/Mascouten, Wea, Shawnee, and Potawatomi were removed in the 1820s and 1830s. The Miami agreed to remove in 1840 and were removed in 1846. It is almost breathtaking—in only two generations the "Land of the Indians" became the land of the other ethnic groups covered in the Peopling Indiana Series.

One might assume at this point that the story of Indiana's original ethnic groups is over, but they continue. Removals were not complete. For example, the Miami had some families exempted from removal by either treaty or resolution. They had land resources in the form of individual allotments granted by treaty and one small communal reservation. Miami individuals or families who avoided removal or who returned to Indiana from the West augmented the numbers of exempted families. This base formed a compact group that achieved federal recognition separate from the western "removed" contingent and thus had a separate history. As removal progressed throughout the eastern United States and as the frontier moved west, the Miami of Indiana became a somewhat isolated group existing behind the frontier. To analyze the challenges to their survival over the next 150 years of post-removal existence, in this volume the Miami of Indiana are compared to another exempted group, the Pokagon Potawatomi of Michigan and Indiana, whose headquarters has been in southern Michigan. The struggles for members of both of these groups has been to retain their rights and identities as Native Americans, their few land resources, and the recognition from the federal government to protect those rights, identities, and lands. This they have had to do through the vicissitudes of ever-changing national Indian policy.

There were also individuals and families from other tribes who escaped the dragnet of removal and who often became known locally as Indian "survivors" or who merged eventually into the majority culture while retaining a personal or family history of Indian identity. To systematically look at those individuals or small groups who also remained behind is more difficult. Some of the small groups have continued to exist in enclaves until the present time, with some retention of traditions and interaction with other Indian groups or activities in the area. Many more were individuals who, for the long period of time when it was not in vogue to have a native background, gradually lost all but the memory that they had Indian ancestry. Sadly, their descendants no longer can fix that identity on a specific tribe or family so that they can focus their pride of heritage.

A third Native American presence comes from individuals and families who belong to tribes from other areas. Initially they came to Indiana during its industrial expansion in the late nineteenth century and continued to come into the twentieth century. These were people who came primarily from the southeast, immigrating in search of work. A large proportion of these individuals identify themselves as Cherokee. A later and much more general immigration has taken place during the late twentieth and into the twenty-first century, so that at present Indiana has an ever-growing population of Native Americans, many from recognized tribes, from every part of the United States. Whereas the Miami are still concentrated along the Wabash River and its tributaries in and around towns such as Peru, Wabash, Huntington, and Marion, recent immigrants are concentrated in urban areas in and around Indianapolis, from Elkhart to Indiana's western border in the north, and in and around Fort Wayne and Evansville. Some active in the Native American community say Indiana has one of the highest proportions of Indian immigration of any state. This seems extraordinary since Indiana is not on the Bureau of Indian Affairs' relocation list. It seems a phenomenon based on word of mouth, dedicated individuals who help with job searches, and, at long last, a social climate comfortable for Native Americans.

So, the authors present more than a three-hundred-year history in this volume. In some ways it is a story of a people adapting to extraordinary conditions and in others a story of their many attempts to retain their land and traditions. At some points it is also a tragic story of, to use some modern terminology, ethnic cleansing. Running through it all is the theme of various strategies for persistence against the odds. Modern increase and diversity make Indiana, in a different way than when it began, the "Land of the Indians."

1

The Original Ethnic Groups of Indiana, 9500 BC–1670 AD

Indiana

Meaning: The Land of Indians
Motto: The Crossroads of America

In 1679 René-Robert Cavalier, Sieur de La Salle, led the first recorded expedition of Euro-Americans into what was to become Indiana. When the expedition had descended the St. Joseph River to its portage with the Kankakee River, one member, Father Louis Hennepin, reported, "This place is situated on the edge of a great plain, at the extremity of which on the western side is a village of Miamis, Mascontens and Oiatinon gathered together."[1] This simple statement is the first mention of ethnic groups different than any other in the Peopling Indiana Series—the Native Americans or American Indians, who were in Indiana before all others.

From 1668 to 1673 the French received indirect information about peoples along the Ohio River in the southern extremity of the state. La Salle learned in 1668 from the Iroquois in the northeast that "this river [Ohio] took its rise three days' journey from Seneca, that after a month's travel one came upon the Honniasontkeronons and the Chiouanons, and that, after passing the latter, and a great cataract or waterfall, one found the Outagame and the Iskousogos."[2] Jacques Marquette and Louis Jolliet, traveling down the Mississippi River, reported passing the mouth of the Ohio (Ouaboukigou) River and elaborated on its population: "This river flows from the lands of the East, where dwell the people called Chaouanons in so great numbers that in one district there are as many as 23 villages, and 15 in another, quite near one another. They are not at all warlike, and are the nations whom the Iroquois go so far to seek, and war against without any reason."[3]

These brief early accounts about Native Americans in Indiana belie the complexity of that earlier history and of later history. They do suggest what peoples resided in Indiana at the time of the first recorded European contact, namely the Miami, Wea, and Mascouten in the extreme north and, most likely, the Shawnee (Chiouanons) in the extreme south. The French already knew the Miami, Wea, and Mascouten through contact earlier in the seventeenth century in present-day Wisconsin. Until displaced into Illinois the French had never met but had only heard about the Shawnee people from other Indians east of or at the mouth of the Ohio River.

It would be almost fifty years after La Salle's exploration before the French would establish permanent posts in what is now Indiana and provide a fuller historical record of the indigenous peoples. To conjecture about Native American peoples in Indiana prior to La Salle's expedition, the archaeological investigation of the region's prehistory is necessary. Although too little space prevents other than a cursory description of this prehistory, the following brief four-part review will at least give an impression of the time span of the Native American occupation in Indiana and some notion of the major cultural developments.[4]

Paleo-Indian period (ca. 9500–8000 BC)

The first opportunity for human occupation within the present state limits occurred as the ice packs of the Wisconsin glaciation receded. At that time small, nomadic, hunting-intensive groups utilized the area's resources. The primary artifactual evidence for this early Paleo-Indian occupation in the state today is a wide distribution of fluted spear points.[5]

Archaic period (ca. 8000–1000 BC)

During the transition to modern climatic conditions, varied cultural adaptations occurred. These cultural responses have been grouped into two major patterns: those who lived mostly in the northern coniferous forests called northern boreal archaic cultures (such as the Glacial Kame, Red Ochre, and Old Copper cultures) and southern shell midden sites. Both the cultures and the sites show more generalized hunting and gathering in a smaller area with a more varied diet than the previous period in which big game hunting over vast acreage was prevalent. In the north smaller, perhaps more nomadic, populations are known primarily by their burial sites. This period is demonstrated in the south by large shell midden sites, deposits of cultural refuse with an obvious dependence on eating mussels. During the late Archaic period, as climatic conditions became more like those in the present day, more complex features associated with burial practices and plant domestication began to develop and continued into the next period.

Early (Adena) and Middle Woodland period (ca. 1000 BC–900 AD)

The hallmarks of this prehistoric phase are earthworks, burial mounds, pottery, and established horticulture. By far the most noted sites from this era are conical burial mounds, with and without internal tombs, and widespread earthwork complexes. This lengthy and diverse period was characterized by intense cultural activity and widespread exchange networks, and burial ritual was a dominant theme of that activity. Recent work in archaeoastronomy, illustrated by earthwork/mound orientation, has added a new interpretative dimension to that cultural intensity.[6] The Mounds State Park in Anderson, Indiana, exemplifies this period.

Middle Mississippian/Late Woodland/Upper Mississippian period (ca. 900 AD to contact)

This is a complex period characterized by a variety of archaeological phenomena. Part of the variety is caused by the number of influences from surrounding states and beyond that overlap Indiana. In southwestern Indiana one finds Middle Mississippian groups with affinities to the southwest; in east central Indiana, the Upper Mississippian Fort Ancient is found with associations to the east. In central Indiana the Oliver Phase is found with associations to the northeast, northwest, and southeast; Upper Mississippian Oneota materials are found in the northwest; and northern Late Woodland expressions are found in the north. With the exception of the extreme north, few cultural generalizations can be made about this complex period. Horticulture is intensive, and the bow and arrow becomes the projectile tool of preference. In addition, settlements, which sometimes had defensive fortifications around them, are larger than in preceding periods. Angel Mounds near Evansville, Indiana, is an interesting example of a fortified Middle Mississippian site dominated by a temple mound.[7]

Historic Period

From the archaeological period preceding contact, one would hope to find evidence of continuity from prehistory to known historic tribes so that specific peoples could be traced both backward and forward in time. The effects of the period on these peoples were, unfortunately, too great to make such assignments with certainty. Diseases introduced in even such far-off localities as the Southeast and Atlantic coasts could travel trade routes to the interior, causing epidemics and unrecorded changes in demography. Trade goods gradually replaced local technologies, and the competition for trade goods caused unrecorded relocations of peoples. Trade and demographic factors also "reconfigured" peoples; that is, groups became extinct, fragmented, recombined, and renamed. These factors, combined with too few well-known transitional sites that can be associated with both an archaeological tradition and a known historic tribe, make assignments difficult. Even the oft-given associations between some of late Fort Ancient with the Shawnee and the eastern expression of Oneota with the Miami and/or Illinois have been called into question.[8] Despite this equivocation, the Miami, or their predecessors, were the most likely occupants of northern Indiana as one enters the period of recorded

PHOTO BY AMY JOHNSON; COURTESY OF DNR, DIVISION OF HISTORIC PRESERVATION AND ARCHAEOLOGY

A portion of the earthworks at Angel Mounds near Evansville in 2008

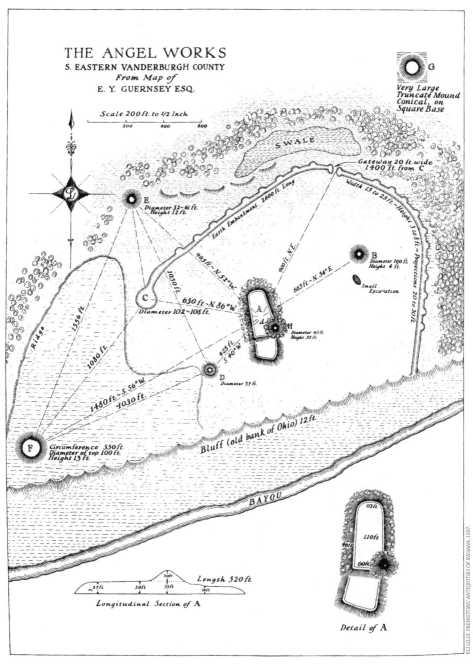

A nineteenth-century drawing of Angel Mounds near Evansville, Indiana, before the site was disrupted by extensive agriculture and excavation in the twentieth century

history, and most late-prehistoric materials in the state were probably associ-ated with Central Algonquian-speaking peoples.

The Central Algonquian language family has been broken down into seven languages: Cree, Ojibwa, Menominee, Miami-Illinois, Potawatomi, Sauk-Fox-Kickapoo, and Shawnee.[9] Most Cree, Ojibwa, and Menominee speakers were distributed north of Indiana and had little relationship to its history. The remainder of the Central Algonquian languages has had at least some impact on the Native American composition of the state during the historic period. Most integral to the state's Native American history are the Miami speakers of the Miami-Illinois language. The Miami proper and the closely related Wea and Piankashaw prevailed throughout the French, British, and early American history of the state and the Miami proper until the present day. Potawatomi speakers were certainly integral to the history of northern Indiana from the mid-eighteenth century. The Fox-Sauk-Kickapoo language was represented in the west-central part of the state by occupants of Kickapoo villages and the Mascouten, thought to be linguistically related, from the 1720s to 1830s. Pos-sible Shawnee villages were located in southern Indiana by the earliest explor-ers and continued to be found in central and southern Indiana sporadically in the eighteenth and early nineteenth centuries.

Many non-Central Algonquian speakers traversed the state through the displacement of groups normally located east and north of the area. Most important of those who actually located here for a substantial period between the 1780s and 1820 were the Eastern Algonquian Delaware and associated Nanticoke. Others, who briefly established villages near Prophetstown in the early nineteenth century, were the Siouan Winnebago, the Muskogean Creek, and the Iroquoian Wyandot. Interesting, if temporary, residents were the Eastern Algonquian Mahican and Iroquoian Huron.

The general cultural pattern of the Central Algonquians that was destined to be affected by European exploration, trade, wars, missionary efforts and, eventually, settlement was adapted to the area and shared broadly with other native occupants of the northeast. Before launching into the cultural pressures of the historic period, it might be well to have a thumbnail sketch of that pattern.[10]

The names listed above, i.e., Miami, Wea, Piankashaw, Potawatomi, Kicka-poo, Mascouten, and Shawnee, as the early native component of the state is a listing of languages or dialects. These language groupings are often morphed into tribal names implying political units. This nation-state view of the world can cause one to overlook the fact that these were kin-based societies where the organizing principle was the kin group (lineage, clan, and so forth) into which one was born. The kin groups were totemic (each group associated with a particular totem object as its emblem), and kinship terminology indicates that all of these groups were patrilineal (both males and females belonged to the kin group of their father), although with the pressures of the historical period, there was a tendency toward bilateralism (descent through both parents). Through one's kin group, parameters of economic, social, and ritual responsibility and behavior were defined; leadership positions and property were inherited; eligibility of marriage partners was delineated; and residence after marriage, and thus the core composition of multifamily households, was determined.

A kinship principle important to this area was moiety. All these societies except for the Shawnee were divided, usually by combining kin groups, into two parts. This duality further defined obligations and behavior. Therefore, these groups were organized in more of a bottom-up web of kin and marriage interrelations than in a top-down, politically organized fashion. Tribal fission (separation or division) was easy and relatively frequent, fusion (merger or unification) was possible by amalgamating or incorporating kin groups, and individual admission to the group was by adoption into a relevant kin group. The Miami-Wea-Piankashaw split is an example of fission, the Kickapoo-Mascouten absorption is an example of fusion, and examples of adoption of both Indians and whites are too numerous to mention.

Contributing to a sense of political fluidity, all the more southern Central Algonquians were semisedentary peoples who moved seasonally (both winter and summer) from established village sites around which they grew their horticultural products. A lack of domesticated herd animals necessitated seasonal moves designed to supplement the staples of maize, beans, and squash with game, fish, and gathered non-domesticated plants acquired on summer and winter hunts. Village sites also moved within their territory as the fertility of fields diminished. The tasks of "making a living" were divided (with some overlap) between males and females, with the women traditionally the horticulturalists and gatherers and the men the hunters and trappers. Access to resources was by usufruct, or temporary right, with one's village, band, or tribe often a determining factor to that access, although what was garnered from that resource was one's own to use or share.

Thus the economy was nearly self-sufficient, with available resources shared by all with group membership rights to them. Therefore groups had a strong sense of territory, and within that territory were located villages surrounded by horticultural resources and locations favorable for hunting, fishing, gathering, and finding resources necessary for tools, utensils, weapons, clothing, and housing. Production also emphasized use of available resources such as stone, hides, furs, bone, horn, shell, soil, wood, and plants to make the necessary tools, weapons, utensils, vehicles, residences, and clothing by a household's "jack-of-all-trades" replication of known technology. At the same time, the superior talents of specialists within communities, such as potters, hunters, and orators, were appreciated by demand. This cultural self-sufficiency was also ameliorated somewhat by what are known to be far-reaching trade networks, along which prized luxury goods, such as copper, fine chert or obsidian, mica, and salt-water mollusk shells, and, sometimes, necessities were traded. Both far-flung networks and nearby resource sharing between groups were made possible by widely understood practices of hospitality and generosity.

Leadership was exercised most frequently at the village rather than the tribal level. All the groups had two leaders at village and tribal levels, a peace

PHOTO BY ELIZABETH BIRKY

Woodland Indians, such as the Miami, Wea, and Potawatomi, built wigwam villages such as these reproduced at Historic Sauder village in Archbold, Ohio.

and a war chief. Often these positions were inherited through a particular lineage. In some groups the leaders consulted with a council, and all were assisted by a "speaker" or "runner." These latter positions also could have been tied to particular lineages. Although the political form was unburdened by complexity, the political process was complex. The process was heavily ritualized, filled with symbolic language, and marked by symbolic paraphernalia (a later example is the calumet or peace pipe). It was also deliberative; the political discussion leading to a decision was designed to consider all aspects of an issue and to reach a consensus, if possible. Beyond the village, band (interrelated group of villages), or tribe (people with shared language and culture), there was also a tendency to create confederation or alliances between groups.

Warfare, the province of the war chief, tended to be for revenge and to achieve war honors. Warfare was frequent, small scale and, for male participants, a part-time enterprise, meaning there were no professional soldiers or standing armies. The war chief organized and planned major war parties, and his and their success depended on surprise and returning with no casualties or few casualties and evidence of damage to the enemy (enemy captives being a prized piece of evidence). Captives either had their courage tested by torture or, more frequently, were adopted into a family of their captors. Individuals in the war party hoped to distinguish themselves by showing courage under risk.

The spiritual dimension of life was based on the belief in immanent supernatural power, the concept that spiritual power is found throughout the natural world. Spiritual activity was directed to accessing that power to affect a desired end. Spiritual power was often subsumed under the hard-to-define word "manitou." These Central Algonquian groups also had a creator god called variously "Master of Life," "Finisher," or "Great Spirit" and a cosmology defining the sacred relationships between time and space. Each individual sought spiritual power through a vision quest at puberty. From that experience an individual acquired a medicine bundle, songs, and rituals, which were a source of personal power. That power's efficacy was manifested by success. Kin groups also had bundles passed down through generations with songs and rituals applicable to the broader kin group. Religious practitioners were shamans who were healers, interpreters of visions, advisors, and ritual organizers. As horticultural societies, the village or band had ceremonies celebrating the harvest. Many of these groups had a Midewiwin or Medicine Society, a secret graded society that served to preserve many religious and healing traditions during the period of contact with Europeans.

This general cultural pattern would contend with the incoming contact with European nation states whose cultural patterns, motivations, economic objectives, and political ambitions had been and were being cultivated across an ocean. Although Native American culture was never static, after native cultures of the region made contact with the European world, the direction and rate of cultural change accelerated to contend with the needs and offerings first of the French, then the English and Spanish, and lastly, the Americans. The successive initial French desires for furs, souls, a transcontinental route to the Orient, and allies in its "contest for continent," primarily with Great Britain, were all to influence the natives directly and indirectly. As the contest for continent was resolved in Britain's favor in 1760, the same objectives remained, except for missionary efforts, so major cultural adjustments for the tribes in the region were not necessary. However, the United States' desire for land began a dramatically different second cycle of adjustment for Native Americans in the region.[11]

2

France, England, and the Fur Trade, 1670–1783

I see this fine village filled with young men, who are, I am sure, as coura-geous as they are well built; and who will, without doubt, not fear their enemies if they carry French weapons. It is for these young men that I leave my gun, which they must regard as the pledge of my esteem for their valor; they must use it if they are attacked. It will also be more satisfactory in hunting cattle and other animals than are all the arrows that you use. To you who are old men I leave my kettle; I carry it everywhere without fear of breaking it. You will cook in it the meat that your young men bring from the chase, and the food which you offer the Frenchmen who come to visit you."
He tossed a dozen awls and knives to the women, and said to them: "Throw aside your bone bodkins; these French awls will be much easier to use. These knives will be more useful to you in killing Beavers and in cutting your meat than are the pieces of stone that you use." Then throwing to them some ras-sade {beads}: "See; these will better adorn your children and girls than do their usual ornaments." The Miamis said, by way of excuse for not having any beaver-skins, that they had until then roasted those animals.

Nicolas Perrot's sales pitch to the Miami and Mascouten in 1668 as
related by Claude Charles Le Roy, Sieur de Bacqueville et de la Potherie[1]

The primary interaction between the two diverse culture patterns of the European world and the Central Algonquians was through the fur trade—an exchange of European manufactured goods for Native American acquired furs. The French first directly contacted most of the Central Algonquians later to be found in present-day Indiana west of Lake Michigan as the French's east-to-west movement of exploration crossed through the Straits of Mackinac and then, in the mid-seventeenth century, south into Lake Michigan and its drainage area, eastern Wisconsin, northeastern Illinois, northern Indiana, and western to central Michigan. Here the usual occupants of the southern peninsula of Michigan and northern Indiana had taken refuge from the Iroquois, who from the late 1630s through the 1680s attacked northern tribes in what came to be called the Iroquois Beaver Wars in order to dominate the northern fur trade. The exploring French encountered Potawatomi, Miami, Wea, Piankashaw, Kickapoo, and Mascouten villages, separate and in combination, as they moved into Green Bay and the nearby interior.

Later in the seventeenth century, French explorers rounded the southern end of Lake Michigan and crossed northwestern Indiana through the portage of the St. Joseph and Kankakee rivers, finding a Miami/Wea/Mascouten village near the portage. This became the first recorded French and Indian encounter in present-day Indiana and the beginning or continuation of the Central Algonquian reoccupation of that region. As French exploration continued south down the Mississippi River, their territory, by virtue of discovery and settlement, encompassed two provinces, Canada and Louisiana, with the boundary between the two crossing Indiana near Terre Haute. Thus present-day Indiana became part of the French colonial system from the late 1600s until 1760.

The French used the waterways as highways for exploration, trade, and an accompanying missionary effort. French trade was organized as a national enterprise through licensed traders and their voyageurs and coureurs de bois. France's early centers of control in the Upper Great Lakes were Michilimackinac and, after 1701, Detroit. Montreal and Quebec on the St. Lawrence River were important but somewhat more distant. Even more distant was New Orleans, the administrative center for Louisiana after 1722. From their centers the French established posts that were licensed to traders, sometimes fortified with a military presence and sometimes served by a nearby mission. The French encouraged the Indians to settle near their centers and posts to ensure trade fidelity and to act as buffers against the British and their Indian allies. In Indiana those posts were Fort Ouiatenon (1717), Fort Miamis (1721), and Fort Vincennes (1732) in the midst of the Wea (later joined by Kickapoo and Mascouten), the Miami proper, and the Piankashaw, respectively. The Potawatomi were served by Fort St. Joseph near present-day Niles, Michigan. At these posts or in the Indian villages the traders, voyageurs, and coureurs de bois traded their goods for furs (preferably in the early spring when the animals had denser winter coats), transported them to a major center, received their profit or salary, and were allotted their consignment of goods for the next season. Such was the French trade.

The diaspora of the seventeenth century also affected residents of the Ohio Valley, such as the Shawnee. The Shawnee dispersed south and east to areas dominated by the British sphere of the New World, giving them a different contact situation from the other Central Algonquians. The British, and Dutch before them, approached the trade as a commercial as opposed to a national enterprise. Initiatives for trade came from colonies, with New York and Pennsylvania having easy access to Indiana by way of both rivers in the Ohio Valley drainage system and the Lower Great Lakes. Native Americans in Indiana also could travel as far as Oswego or Albany in New York to trade. The cheaper, higher quality, and more diverse British trade goods made it worth their while, and so the Shawnee were not the only area residents in contact with that outlet throughout the early and mid-eighteenth century. After the French and Indian War (1754–60), the British took over French posts and networks of the Upper Great Lakes and maintained their authority from 1760 to 1783. The fur trade of the area, still run at the basic level by the pre-existing French network, did not change much.

The importance of Indiana to the French was threefold. It provided a supply of fur-bearing animals, although not as prime as those further north. Native Americans not only provided those furs, but were also important allies in the "contest for continent" with the English. Indiana also provided important portages that effectively connected the drainages of the Great Lakes and Mississippi River and thus the two French provinces.

La Salle's 1679 exploration took a route through the northwestern corner of future Indiana using a portage near present-day South Bend connecting the St. Joseph and Kankakee rivers and thus Lake Michigan and the Mississippi River. During the early eighteenth century, the French surely became aware of other routes in the state that would create useful connections: the Maumee River (Little River)/Wabash River portage near Fort Wayne, the Maumee River/Eel River portage near Fort Wayne, the Elkhart River/St. Joseph of the Maumee portage in Noble County, and the St. Joseph of Lake Michigan/Tippecanoe River portage. The Maumee River portages, especially the Maumee/Wabash at Fort Wayne, were particularly important because, starting from Lake Erie, they provided a route that avoided the northern trip up through the Straits of Mackinac and thus more directly connected French centers in Canada with the Louisiana province. The Miami, Wea, and Mascouten were first found at the St. Joseph/Kankakee portage. During the 1710s to 1730s, various tribes aligned themselves along the Maumee/Wabash passage with the Miami in their village Kekionga (Fort Miamis) near the portage, the Wea/Mascouten/Kickapoo at Ouiatenon (near Lafayette), and the Piankashaw at Vincennes. The Potawatomi gradually occupied the St. Joseph/Kankakee area vacated earlier by the Miami. Thus French, Indians, and later, the British responded to the waterway-dominated topography of the fur trade.

This portion of a 1688 map of western New France by Vincenzo Coronelli, although somewhat inaccurate, shows Indian settlements around Lake Michigan (Lac des Illinois/Lac Dauphin), including Miami and Potawatomi Indian villages, at the end of the seventeenth century.

A basic problem exists in assessing how the Native Americans in the Upper Great Lakes responded to this European initiative and framework. Because the Indians were preliterate, information about them is dependent on the relatively sparse and culturally biased record left by the European explorers, traders, missionaries, administrators, and soldiers. Thus information about population numbers of the various groups encountered and details about their cultures, interrelationships, movements, and motivations has to be reconstructed with caution from multiple, often contradictory, sources.[2]

One self-evident aspect of this cultural contact is the Native American acceptance of the exchange itself. The fur trade was an economic venture involving a reciprocal relationship between the incoming Europeans and the indigenous peoples. Simply stated, the fur trade depended on the Native American as the trapper of furs and on his willingness to exchange those furs for European manufactured goods, primarily made of metal, cloth, and glass.[3] This was an exchange process that began, for North America, by the sixteenth century. The demand of each side was so great for what the other provided that some effects of European trade on Native Americans living in the interior of the continent preceded actual contact. As the fur trade moved west with the French in the latter half of the seventeenth century, its direct influence was profound. The introduction of European manufactured metal-edged tools and utensils, metal containers (such as kettles), cloth, muskets, glass beads, and other standard stock of the early trade in exchange for furs and hides presented a highly desirable choice for the Native Americans. Most obviously it disrupted, in time, traditional technological production through the replacement of metal for stone, wood, antler, and bone tools and weapons; of metal kettles for clay, wood, bark, or leather containers; and, as furs and skins were the primary trade item, of cloth and blankets for leather and fur clothing and robes. Decorative or luxury items were no less affected. Glass beads, ribbons, and metal ornaments replaced shell, porcupine quill, and stone decorative elements for personal or clothing adornment. The introduction of new, not replacement, commodities (such as guns and alcohol) controversially became other staples of the trade cycle.[4]

Initially, a preference for the new materials that could neither be made nor repaired by the traditional economy drove the trade, and much later, when plentiful trade goods caused a loss of traditional technology, a dependency on the trade was created. Thus a new economic adaptation developed, directed away from self-sufficiency and toward the acquisition of goods both made and controlled by another cultural tradition and the fluctuations of a distant market system. As dependency on the trade became established, indebtedness ensued, and even more furs or services could be demanded to eradicate the debt. Moreover, as male economic activities became directed increasingly to acquiring necessities through fur trading, their absenteeism enhanced women's economic and management functions for both the households and the village. One can also imagine that as the trade became established, labor-intensive tasks such as making pottery or fashioning beads out of stone and shell were replaced by tasks such as preparing furs and hides, in order to maximize the return from the fur trade.

The acceptance of the fur trade by the Native Americans did not necessarily mean that all items were accepted, that they were used as intended by their European originators, or that the recipients treated the items as having only material value. After the novelty of European goods wore off, all groups became quite discriminating about their choices, and unless the trader wanted to return with untraded goods, he catered to those tastes. Preferences could include factors such as color, style, quality, and weight. These preferences even went back to production—whole lines of products were manufactured specifically for the trade. In the hands of the Native American, these goods were translated into their own sense of style and taste. This was most evident in apparel and bodily adornment. Blankets became robes; colorful strips of cloth became turbans; silver was in demand as wrist and arm bands, elaborate nose and ear ornaments, cascading pendants, or was sewn onto clothing or headgear; ribbons and beads were rendered into intricate designs; and even "ready-made" clothing was worn or transformed according to individual or cultural style.

The far-reaching influences of the trade could also be seen in a social sphere of native culture due to the openness of their societies and driven by the need to regularize access to trade goods. Individually and locally the most common way to structure ties for both the French and Indians was by intermarriage between the trader in the field and a daughter of an often-prominent member of the tribe. Initially, intermarriage created strong primary relationships for trading purposes. In subsequent generations a large population of Métis (mixed-blood) developed in the Great Lakes region. The Métis population often became specialists in the trade and, as the trade diminished, played integral roles as members of Great Lakes tribes.

Access to the trade also affected general demography. Indian villages or bands became tied to locations of trading posts or other outlets for goods. That relocation was often tied to access to better, cheaper goods or to the manipulation of the French and English in creating buffer areas from each other. An important exception existed in what was to become Indiana. As the Miami and Wea were settling on the Wabash passage during the early eighteenth century, the French wanted them to move north to protect the French settlements of Detroit and St. Joseph. The Miami and Wea refused this invitation to be nearer the French and stayed at their locations near present-day Fort Wayne and Lafayette.[5] This refusal led in part to the French establishing their Indiana posts at those locations.

Some tribes adopted new political and strategic objectives, such as a middleman role in the trade network. The middleman position existed when a tribe had the finesse to impose itself between the European trader and tribes who had furs but not direct access to a trade outlet. This put the middleman tribe in a position to control access to prime goods, using furs from the territories of others. It also enhanced the tribe's political position within its region of influence.

Early in the St. Lawrence trade first the Montagnais and then the Huron held such a position. The Five Nation Iroquois aspired to such a position as prime furs became scarce in their territory, and their failure contributed to the Iroquois Beaver Wars when aggression was substituted for trade finesse. As the French made contact with potential trading partners in present-day Wisconsin, they first encountered the Potawatomi, who attempted to monopolize the French but were thwarted when the French bypassed them to meet with the Miami, Mascouten, Kickapoo, and others directly.[6] As French exploration and tribal movement entered Indiana, an interesting and long-lasting middleman relationship developed. By 1669–70 the Mahican, an Eastern Algonquian tribe from the Hudson River region of New York, gained permission to trade for furs in the Miami and Ottawa territories. Again in 1680 two bands of River Indians (Mahican and Esopus) went west to trade among the Miami. By 1687 the Five Nation Iroquois asked the Mahican to intercede on their behalf with the Miami to end the hostilities of the Beaver Wars, and, as late as 1721, a group of Mahican settled in the Kankakee region.[7] Mahican middlemen gave the Miami access to the Dutch/British trade, which offered cheaper and better goods than the French, and in turn the Miami became middlemen within their region of influence. From the viewpoint of the French, this meant the Miami and other Wabash groups had access to the British, and as early as the 1720s the Miami were traveling as far as Albany to trade.

Thus, just the simple idea of exchange, the fur trade, created a context of change for the native cultures of Indiana. They had access to goods outside of their production capability for a commodity they were experts at finding, trapping, and processing. This changed the emphasis of their traditional, self-sufficient economy. To ensure continuing access to those goods, Native Americans located their villages near posts or river passages, used marriage as a trade alliance strategy, and adopted distinctive styles enabled by the trade. They also had their own strategies for success in dealing with the new opportunity. They could gain an advantage by achieving a middleman position, and they could play one market against another (France and Great Britain) to get better exchanges.

Although trade dominated the French contact period economically, the missionary effort was also of great importance to French goals. Irrespective of its importance to the French, conversion from traditional beliefs to Catholicism did not have the same immediate allure to the Native Americans as conversion from stone to metal tools. Despite the effort of numerous missionaries from various orders, the success rate of actual conversion was low. Early baptisms were heavily biased toward infants, the sick and dying, and Indian spouses of French traders. More frequently, an apparent acceptance of a Christian doctrine, rite, or belief was characterized by a superficial understanding or immanent interpretation of the transcendent Christian doctrine. Because Native Americans possessed a belief system that emphasized the acquisition of supernatural power that manifested through success in an endeavor such as hunting or raising crops, a Christian ritual, artifact, or medicine would be adopted in isolation of the larger Catholic religion if it, too, appeared to manifest power through success in one of life's endeavors. Thus strong cultural effects of the vigorous missionary effort were not to appear until much later in the contact period. This was particularly true in present-day Indiana. Although there were long-lasting missions in Wisconsin, Michigan, and Illinois, there were none in Indiana.[8] Individual missionaries attended the needs of the inhabitants and Indian converts of Forts Vincennes, Ouiatenon, and Miamis somewhat inconsistently.

Protestant missionaries, active in the British colonies, had a more indirect impact. Unlike the Catholic mission effort in the Upper Great Lakes, the

[Handwritten French contract, 1721]

Under the terms of this 1721 contract, trader Charles Fabereau was to deliver supplies to Sieur Dumont, commander of the Miamis post (now Fort Wayne) and to deliver Dumont's fur pelts to Montreal for sale.

Protestant missionaries were not tied to a trade system that in many ways
did not want to change the way of life that provided the furs. One approach
of the eastern Protestant effort was to isolate converts from their "heathen"
brethren and not only convert them to Christianity but culturally "westernize"
them; examples include the Moravian missionary villages of Schoenbrunn and
Gnadenhutten in eastern Ohio. Another approach was the emotional impact
of the evangelical revival. The Delaware, a later arrival in Indiana, experienced
both an extensive missionizing by the Moravians and the evangelical experience. The Shawnee were less influenced than the Delaware by these experiences, as they moved in and out of Indiana and the east but were active with
those who were being influenced by missionary concepts in the multitribal
villages in Pennsylvania and Ohio.

Trade and mission efforts were directed toward the Native American,
and both were sustained by control of the region by one or another European
power. Competition for control also became a concern of the region's Indians.
Native Americans were used as auxiliaries by Britain's colonial armies and, as
each contest between France and Britain became more intense, the regional
tribes, separately or in combination, could choose to ally with one of the powers for political and trade leverage. In this multifaceted interaction with various Euro-American interests, the duality of Indian leadership (the presence of
separate civil and war leaders) was evidently an advantage, since it persisted
through much of the early contact period.

The major and usually inadvertent influence on Native Americans introduced by the explorers, European traders, missionaries, politicians, and
soldiers was disease. Measles, mumps, chicken pox, smallpox, and tuberculosis, to name a few, were diseases previously unknown in the New World, and
because of this, no immunity to them had developed in its indigenous populations. Several epidemics in the Upper Great Lakes/Ohio River region had devastating results. Smallpox epidemics swept through tribes in Indiana in 1733,
1752, 1757, 1762–64, 1781–82, 1787–88, and 1801. The Wea had a measles
epidemic in 1715, and scarlet fever affected the Miami and Potawatomi in
1793–94.[9] Particularly vulnerable were the very old (the tradition carriers) and
the very young (the strength of the next generation), with destructive effects
on a tribe's ability to sustain both a culture and a population. Often, so many
people were sick at a given time that the ability to carry on the normal pattern
of life was impossible. During the measles epidemic in 1715, the Wea were
unable to fulfill their military obligations to the French. The smallpox

epidemic of 1733 caused the Miami to abandon their towns and disperse into northern Indiana.[10]

Another major influence was alcohol, which was purposefully introduced, even after its harmful affects on Native Americans were well known. Used by traders to undersell their competition and by politicians to gain concessions, alcohol became an uncontrollable commodity.

Native Americans of this region responded with change and adaptation to the elements purposefully and inadvertently introduced to them—trade, religion, European warfare and alliances, disease, and alcohol. However, responses also indicated that all was not well with the status quo. The economic competition between France and Britain itself became an instrument of change for the area's tribes. Alliances shifted as portions of groups such as the Miami, Wea, Piankashaw, and Shawnee dealt with the British, while the Potawatomi remained relatively constant in their French alliance.

Another type of response was an anti-French movement led by the Wyandot (Huron/Petun) chief Nicolas (aka Orontony, Sanosket). Leaving the Detroit region in 1738, Nicolas and his band settled at Sandusky, Ohio. Pennsylvania traders established a trade blockhouse among them in 1745. From that region, Nicolas tried to rally the area's tribes, including the Miami and others, into a pan-Indian force to drive the French out. It was to be a coordinated intertribal action in August 1747, but had minimal success because the French were forewarned.[11] Some Miami who were allies of Nicolas and led by La Demoiselle (Old Briton) pillaged and burned the French post, Fort Miamis, and captured its French occupants. La Demoiselle was ultimately thwarted by pro-French Miami, who persuaded him to release the captives and then requested French reinforcements.[12]

In 1748 Nicolas destroyed his village and the trading blockhouse at Sandusky and moved his followers (120 warriors and their families) to the White River in Indiana. The same year Nicolas died as the group traveled further west.[13] La Demoiselle moved with his band of Miami to present-day Piqua, Ohio, and formed an active pro-British trading community, Pickawillany. To further formalize his break with the French, in 1748 La Demoiselle sent a contingent from his band to Pennsylvania, where three of his followers, including his son, signed a treaty of alliance with the British.[14] The remainder of the Miami, under Le Pied Froid and Le Gris, remained in present-day Indiana. This split of the Miami persisted until 1752, when a French/Indian force destroyed Pickawillany and killed La Demoiselle.

As the area's trade competition merged into the military competition that was the French and Indian War, the majority of the tribes of the region realigned themselves with their old friends, the French. However, when Britain achieved dominance over Canada at the end of the war in 1760, former Indian allies of the French discovered the disadvantage of both a noncompetitive trading situation and alliance with the losing side. The French practice of giving presents and goods to maintain Indian loyalty and goodwill was discontinued by the British, who considered it an unnecessary expense. The end of hostilities also encouraged the illegal movement of British colonists west, exposing Indian lands to a new threat. The Indians responded in 1763 with Pontiac's War. Similar to Chief Nicolas's military adventure a few years before, the Ottawa chief Pontiac organized a pan-Indian response to the European presence in the region, with a coordinated force planning to strike all the European posts at the same time. This action was nearly successful—of all the posts in the northwest, only Forts Detroit and Pitt were able to hold. Along the Maumee-Wabash passage only Forts Miamis and Ouiatenon had been occupied by small British forces, and both fell quickly during the uprising. Ensign Robert Holmes at Miamis was persuaded to leave the fort, was shot, and his

Silver items, such as these bracelets, were in high demand in the fur trade.

men surrendered. At Ouiatenon, Lieutenant Edward Jenkins was taken captive, and his men surrendered.[15] The Miami, Kickapoo, Mascouten, Wea, and, indirectly, the Potawatomi seem to have been involved in these actions.

Although initially successful, the pan-Indian alliance was unable to sustain this uprising. Taking Forts Detroit and Pitt required a long siege, which was not an Indian tactic. Also, deteriorating economic conditions were exacerbated by a smallpox epidemic introduced from Fort Pitt. These factors brought home to the Upper Great Lakes tribes the reality of their continued dependency, engendered by a century of involvement in the European-controlled fur trade/alliance system. However, the widespread military successes of the Native Americans during Pontiac's War also demonstrated to the British their own vulnerability as a small minority in Indian lands. British authorities attempted to regularize trade and, through the Proclamation of 1763, to establish a boundary between colonists and Indian country.

Another internal response to the European presence came through religion. Primarily as a response produced by contact with the Protestant missionaries in the East, a number of Indian seers and prophets arose during the mid-eighteenth century, especially among the Munsee and Unami Delaware. Those who had a far-reaching affect prior to 1763 were Papoonan (1752), Wangomend (Assisinsink prophet) (1752), and Neolin (1761). The Delaware had lost their east coast lands and had begun their migration westward, coming into contact with many clients of the multitribal trading centers in Pennsylvania and Ohio. Just as trade goods were exchanged, so were ideas and solutions to the problems now becoming generally perceived by a broad base of the Native American population.

One solution was the kind of nativistic movement the Delaware prophets advocated. Taken from the Christian message on the importance of the Bible to Europeans and the judgmental and punitive aspects of heaven and hell, two concepts emerged in the Indian community—that there were three creations, each separate with beliefs particular to Indians, blacks, and Europeans, and that Indians were being punished and would be punished in the afterlife for not preserving the spiritual power of their creation if that state were not rectified. Acceptance of trade goods (especially alcohol) and the diminishing of the old ways of achieving power became a causal factor for their deplorable state after a century of the fur trade. Each of the movements begun by the three prophets named above was initiated by a visionary experience, and each advocated separation from trade dependency, giving up alcohol, and the practice of old (sometimes revised) rituals. For the Indiana Native Americans, Neolin's vision became the most widespread, especially among some Potawatomi and Miami. His vision was also of interest to Pontiac, thus joining the spiritual and military reaction to European incursion.[16]

Once the disruption of Pontiac's War was stabilized, the changes for the Native Americans were not that extensive during the brief British domination. The fur trade continued, still run, insofar as concerned the Indians, by the French and Métis intermediaries with whom they usually did business. The Spanish, just across the Mississippi River, offered another trade option, providing a nearby market and political alternative. However, conflict again rose in the last third of this brief period. As the pressure of colonists became greater along the Ohio River and as the American colonies moved toward revolution against Britain, the Indians were again drawn into conflict. Since by now they perceived their lands threatened by the ambitions of the Americans, this time they fought in the interests of the British, which were in fact their own interests.

Throughout the fur trade period, the French and British made only a small footprint in what was to be Indiana. Counts done by the British indicate that in 1767 Vincennes had 232 inhabitants (men, women, and children) and 168 transients; in 1769, it had 266 inhabitants. Ouiatenon had 12 inhabitants and Fort Miamis 9 in 1769 (neither counting families).[17] There were no missions in what was to become Indiana, and military presence at the posts varied with necessity, but large forces were never posted for a period of time. In short, present-day Indiana was still Indian territory, as it had been throughout the French and British period. However, European members of this small footprint introduced directed cultural changes in material culture, religion, politics, and military activity that far outweighed their numerical proportion. Change occurred that was different than would have occurred in the normal course of affairs.

Another view of this small European footprint is archaeological. However, pursuing an archaeological view has a limitation. Forts Vincennes and Miamis now are covered by urban growth, leaving Ouiatenon as the best available site for archaeological investigation. The location of Ouiatenon was confirmed in the late 1960s, and since that time various crews have surveyed and excavated the site.[18] Even more pertinent to this volume, excavations have expanded into the nearby Wea village and the mixed community of the "jack-knife" post,

Kethtippecanunk.[19] As these data become expanded and analyzed, even more understanding of this era will be available.

The fur trade era lasted more than one hundred years (1654–1783), and changes occurred slowly, allowing for adaptation. Trade goods were introduced, but many were modified to Native American tastes or rejected if they did not suit preexisting tastes or needs. Locations of villages and even tribes shifted to accommodate the trade, but much of the annual cycle of life and many of the activities within these groups changed little. Warfare was probably fought on a larger scale, if not more frequently, in the pursuit of European interests, but by the end of the period it was beginning to be pursued for Indian interests against Europeans. The mission effort had less an effect on converting large numbers to Christianity in this area than in causing the beginning of a rethinking of religious concepts through pan-Indian nativistic movements. Both the militant and nativistic pan-Indian movements cut across traditional kin/tribe identities and indicated a perception that all was not well—the contact situation had somehow gone too far. Contributing to that sense of disruption were other negative introductions of the fur trade—disease and alcohol. However, with the coming of the American Revolution, considerable change was on the horizon.

3

Early American Period, 1783–1812

Brothers—We all belong to one family; we are all children of the Great Spirit; we walk in the same path; slake our thirst at the same spring; and now affairs of the greatest concern lead us to smoke the pipe around the same council fire! Brothers—We are friends; we must assist each other to bear our burdens. The blood of many of our fathers and brothers has run like water on the ground, to satisfy the avarice of the white men. We, ourselves, are threatened with a great evil; nothing will pacify them but the destruction of all the red men. . . .

Brothers—If you do not unite with us, they will first destroy us, and then you will fall an easy prey to them. They have destroyed many nations of red men because they were not united, because they were not friends to each other.

> Tecumseh to the Osage, 1811[1]

For the Native American groups in what would eventually become Indiana, the transition from French/British to American interests in their territory would require a whole new adaptive strategy. Until now the relationship of the Native Americans to the Europeans with whom they came in contact was based on the trade/mission/military complex. This complex involved the Indians as an integral part of the fur trade, as the object of the mission effort, and as necessary allies in the contest for continent. The ultimate American objective was quite different: acquire the land itself for colonization and development by its own citizens, without Indians.

Much has been written about the United States' shifts on Indian policy from demand by right of conquest, to confrontation, to negotiation, all used ultimately for territorial expansion. Much also has been written about the framework of territorial development beginning with the Northwest Ordinance in 1787, through the peopling of Indiana with Anglo-Americans, and the acquisition of statehood under the ordinance.[2] In response to the territorial demands by the United States, Native Americans increasingly were forced to react to events and policies not of their making and often in direct opposition to their interests. To the Indians of Indiana, this was less apparent before the War of 1812 but unquestioned after—a factor that deeply affected their strategies and responses to circumstances in two stages during the period of American control before the Native Americans were forced to move out of the state.

The American Revolution in what is now Indiana included: George Rogers Clark's incursion into the Illinois country, the acquiescence of Vincennes to American occupation, the capture of Vincennes by the British lieutenant governor of Detroit, Henry Hamilton, after his expedition down the Wabash River from Detroit, the retaking of Vincennes by Clark overland through Illinois, and the pro-American expedition by Augustin de La Balme from Vincennes to Fort Miamis and his defeat northwest of that site by the Miami. Although Native Americans negotiated with Clark and accompanied and then left Hamilton, the Vincennes aspect of the conflict was not their affair. The 1780 de La Balme expedition against the trading post and Indian towns at Fort Miamis, however, was their affair and resulted in the total defeat of the expedition by the Miami and their Métis traders led by Little Turtle.[3] The American Revolution in the West ended for the Miami and their confederates on that note. Little wonder that the results of the 1782–83 transatlantic peace negotiations, in which the British relinquished their territory to the United States and the subsequent attitude of Americans about their rights of conquest, were mystifying to the region's Indian population. This was particularly true since, with the exception of the established French/Métis trading communities along the Wabash and the new Clark's Grant at the Falls of the Ohio, Indiana was still the "land of the Indians."

In 1783 the distribution of the American Indian population in the region had not changed dramatically since early in the century. Long-established trading communities drew and held concentrations of Native American populations: the Miami, Delaware, and Shawnee in the area of Kekionga; the Wea and Kickapoo near the dwindling post of Ouiatenon; and the Piankashaw at Vincennes. The Potawatomi were in the north near the St. Joseph and

Kankakee rivers trading posts. Subsidiary trading posts, called "jack-knife" posts, primarily at the mouths of Wabash tributaries, drew concentrations such as the Potawatomi and Wea to Kethtippecanunk and the Miami to Kenapacomaqua, near the mouths of the Tippecanoe and Eel rivers, respectively.[4] Other villages, less reported, existed between the older centers.

Despite the appearance of population stability, three changes in the composition of Native American inhabitants should be noted. Tribes from the former British colonies in the East, having lost their land, traversed this far

GENERAL PICTURE COLLECTION, CA. 1860S-1980S. P 0411, INDIANA HISTORICAL SOCIETY

The Miami War Chief Little Turtle who led both the Miami and an intertribal resistance to military invasions into Indian territory

west. Notable among those exiles were bands of Delaware and a small group
of Nanticoke, both originally from the mid-Atlantic area. Another change was
the more southerly range of Potawatomi settlement as they expanded into
much of the northern third of Indiana. Lastly, groups known to have been
in and around the Indiana region for all or a part of the preceding century
faced extinction or, more often, absorption into other tribes, such as the
assimilation of remnants of the Mascouten by the Kickapoo by the early
nineteenth century.

Throughout the early American period, this heterogeneous population
faced a complex set of circumstances. Within an international context, the
region's Indians had been players in the continental competition between first
France and Great Britain and then Britain and the United States. The French
influence was still present in the trade system and local population. The British
climate still existed in trade and politics. In fact the British, who continued
to occupy Detroit after relinquishing the site in the 1783 peace treaty, were
geographically and politically closer to the region's Indians than if confined to
their Canadian territory. The principal demand of the United States was for

*This painting of the Greenville Treaty by an unknown member of General Anthony Wayne's
staff, ca. 1795, shows Indians, and particularly the famous Little Turtle, negotiating with
Americans, led by Wayne. The Greenville Treaty is of particular importance because it is the
foundational treaty for American Indian rights in the Midwest today, promising fair treatment and legal protection in exchange for land.*

land. The United States' intentions were not lost on the Native Americans of the area and, if that realization should lag, the British were there to remind them.

The Native American response to the threat to their territory was the largest pan-Indian political gathering to date. In the fall of 1783 the Grand Council of the Western Alliance gathered at Sandusky in Wyandot territory. More than thirty tribes were represented, including not only many from what was to be the Northwest Territory but also representatives from the Iroquois and the Southeast. Most active from present-day Indiana were the Miami, Potawatomi, Shawnee, and Delaware. The council sought to be the representative body with which the United States would negotiate and held that the unalterable boundary between Indian and United States lands would be the Ohio River.[5] The United States, considering itself the owner of land north of the Ohio by virtue of conquest, proceeded to hold treaties with a few accommodationist Native Americans to alienate that land from the Native American tribes, and it organized surveys of the land. In response the Grand Council met again in Detroit in December 1786 to denounce the treaties as being signed by unrepresentative individuals, to demand a suspension of the land surveys, and to again assert that the council was the representative body with whom negotiations should be held. The United States, at Fort Harmar in January 1789, reaffirmed the previous treaties with council representatives and partially relinquished the "right of conquest" stand by agreeing to compensate tribes for alienated lands, but still "gave" northwestern tribes portions of U.S. lands they were now allowed to occupy.[6]

The United States continued to direct its diplomacy to establishing a boundary between Euro-American and tribal lands that would open more land for frontier settlement. In another tack, the newly elected president, George Washington, urged on by General Josiah Harmar and Arthur St. Clair, governor of the Northwest Territory, initiated a military response to Indian resistance to the loss of their homeland. American armies and militia under the command of first Harmar and then St. Clair in 1790 and 1791, respectively, invaded the Indians' territory. Meanwhile American militia harassed Indian settlements along the Wabash. The target of the large campaigns and militia harassment was the concentration of Indian villages in the Wabash/Maumee region. Under the Miami war leader Little Turtle, the confederation of Indian tribes that gathered to defend their territory defeated both armies and gave one army, St. Clair's, the most one-sided defeat ever suffered by an American army in an Indian conflict. Smaller militia incursions primarily destroyed recently deserted Indian towns and their surrounding crops.[7]

In the first actual confrontation, Harmar's campaign, Indian strategies, such as luring troops into an ambush by scattering trinkets around a deserted campsite, were sufficient to create disarray in the American army. The result was that an outwitted and disheveled American detachment bolted the battle-field with considerable loss from a much smaller, primarily Miami force. The panic of the detachment was contagious throughout much of the total force. Three days later another American detachment was turned back at the already destroyed Miami, Delaware, and Shawnee towns around present-day Fort Wayne. That finished Harmar's expedition.[8]

The devastation of St. Clair's campaign involved a completely different strategy—frontal attack and encirclement of a set rectangular encampment protected by cannon. This was accomplished by a combined force of Miami, Shawnee, Delaware, Wyandot, Potawatomi, Ottawa, and Chippewa—half the size of the encamped army—that attacked on the morning of November 4, 1791. The loss to the combined Indian force was 21 killed and 40 wounded. St. Clair's losses were 630 killed or missing and 280 wounded out of an on-site force of 1,400. All of the American army's equipment and war material, $33,000 worth, was lost in the precipitous retreat.[9]

Little Turtle is credited as the strategist for the varied approaches used against both Harmar and St. Clair. The Shawnee war leader Blue Jacket and the Delaware Chief Buckongahelas assisted in carrying out the plan against St. Clair. The victors held another Grand Council at the Glaze, near present-day Defiance, Ohio, in September 1792 to consider current conditions. Debate centered upon two major choices: whether these military successes should be followed by driving settlers out of the disputed territory north of the Ohio or whether the military advantage should be used to negotiate a compromised but advantageous peace. Despite long councils that considered promises of support from the English, endured much interference from the Iroquois, and often broke down into tribal self-interest, neither option was pursued. Instead, the old position, the Ohio River as an unalterable boundary, would stand.[10]

The native impasse allowed General Anthony Wayne to prepare a larger, better-trained, and better-equipped army, the Legion of the United States, for the third major invasion of Indian territory. As Wayne marched north from the Cincinnati area in 1793 and 1794, he constructed a line of forts, including Fort Recovery on the site of St. Clair's defeat. Attrition in his ranks occurred, and at times his army or supply line was quite vulnerable. The Indians, however, did not take effective advantage of these weaknesses. As Little Turtle watched Wayne's preparation, he advised against confrontations with this larger, very different army. He became a participant as the more militant Shawnee Blue Jacket assumed command for the conflict that finally took place at Fallen Timbers on August 20, 1794.[11] For his part, Wayne delayed his actual attack until a portion of the Indian force, having fasted for three days waiting for Wayne to act, dispersed to hunt.[12] This brief encounter was a daytime frontal assault on a fixed barricaded line (not an Indian tactic). The battle, lasting only an hour and ten minutes with low and nearly equal losses on each

LEWIS JAMES OTTO, *THE ABORIGINAL PORT FOLIO*, 1836

Tenskwatawa, known as The Prophet

George Washington,

PRESIDENT of the

UNITED STATES of AMERICA,

To all to whom these Presents shall come:

K NOW YE, That the nation of Indians called the *Wiatonon* inhabiting the town of *Wiau* and other towns, villages, and lands of the same community, are, in their persons, towns, villages, lands, hunting-grounds and other rights and property in the peace and under the protection of the United States of America: And all persons, citizens of the United States are hereby warned not to commit any injury, trespass or molestation whatever on the persons, lands, hunting-grounds, or other rights or property of the said Indians: And they and all others are in like manner forbidden to purchase, accept, agree or treat for, with the said Indians directly or indirectly, the title or occupation of any lands held or claimed by them; and I do hereby call upon all persons in authority under the United States, and all citizens thereof in their several capacities, to be aiding and assisting to the prosecution and punishment according to law of all persons who shall be found offending in the premises.

GIVEN under my Hand and the Seal of the United States this *seventh* day of *May* in the year of our Lord one thousand seven hundred and ninety-*three* and of the Independence of the United States of America the *seventeenth*

Presidential decrees, such as this to the Wea in 1793, were issued in an attempt to settle tribes while treaty negotiations proceeded.

side, began with an Indian advantage, but when the legion's lines held and advanced, the Indian force retreated and was then put to rout. They fell back to Fort Miamis, a British fort constructed in the region during the preceding year, to regroup and found the gates closed and locked against them. The Indian coalition broke up completely. Negotiation from a position of strength was no longer an option.[13]

By August 1794, after repeated destruction of Indian crops and villages and an epidemic, the Native Americans of the region were hungry, impoverished, and without provision for the coming winter. The British, upon whom they depended for supplies, did not provide sufficient resources to alleviate the problem. The failure of the British to give the promised military support particularly demoralized the Indians. In fact, once again, events in Europe over which they had no control overtook the Native Americans. In the Jay Treaty, signed in London in 1794, the British agreed to vacate the Northwest Territory forts, leaving the Indians without any nearby economic or military support. These factors, more than the single battle at Fallen Timbers, led to the Treaty of Greenville in 1795, which began the process of alienating Indian lands in what was to be Indiana to the United States government and ended, with the exception of the War of 1812, formal Indian/white warfare in the area.

In the immediate post-Greenville years a proportion of the region's Indians relocated. Fort Wayne and its immediate area now belonged to the United States, and the diversified Indian population at that location began to disperse. The Shawnee moved east into Ohio; the Delaware built a number of villages along the White River; and the Miami moved from Kekionga to the Upper Wabash and its tributaries.

Despite the turmoil and population shifts, the fur trade, now an integral part of the Indian economy, continued. Traders of American origin now competed with pre-existing French and British networks still active in the area. The most notable of these were William Burnett and the Conner brothers, John and William. They used the traditional means of establishing primary connections by intermarriage: William Burnett married Kakima, sister of the influential Potawatomi Topenebee, and William Conner married Mekinges, daughter of the Delaware chief Anderson. Although Burnett had his trading post in Michigan on the St. Joseph River, he sent "adventures" into both the Kankakee and Wabash river drainages. His records give an excellent impression of the trade during that era.[14] The careers of the Conner brothers in central Indiana along the White River are also well documented, and so, expand understanding about trade in central Indiana.[15]

Additionally, the United States government, faced with the economic problems of a new nation, wanted to break into the pre-existing trade networks. The somewhat unique idea was to develop a trade factory system that would trade goods to the Indians for furs in a not-for-profit enterprise, hoping in this way to undersell the other trade networks. This tactic was started in 1795, and in 1801 the first federal factory was established in Indiana at Fort Wayne with John Johnston as the factor. The Fort Wayne factory was among the most successful, demonstrating the continuing importance of furs in the area.[16] Yet just as goods were most plentiful and variable for the Native American and as the trade system was providing information at its fullest for later researchers, the seeds of destruction for the fur trade were at hand—pioneer farmers who would clear and plow the land.

When the Indiana Territory was formed in 1800 and William Henry Harrison was appointed territorial governor, alienation of Indian lands and the rapid settlement of the territory with pioneers were his primary objectives. Harrison inaugurated a series of treaties with the Miami, the Piankashaw, the Wea, the now-independent Eel River Miami, the Kickapoo (and the absorbed Mascouten), the Potawatomi, the Shawnee, and more recent immigrants from the East such as the Delaware (including the Munsee and Nanticoke), the Ottawa, and the Wyandot. The treaties Harrison made between 1803 and 1809 took from Indian control primarily southern portions of present-day Indiana.

The rapidity of land loss, the insidious divide-and-conquer approach to treaty making, and the relatively few Indian leaders involved in the treaties combined to bring about political and religious responses from Native Americans. One political response continued the Grand Council concept. The largest council meetings, involving twelve to thirteen tribes, were held in the Kickapoo town near Lafayette in 1807; at Parc aux Vaches, near present-day Bertrand, Michigan, on the St. Joseph River in 1810; and at Mississinewa in May 1812. Peace and war chiefs attended not only from the Indiana tribes but also from the Wyandot, Winnebago, Ottawa, and Chippewa tribes.[17] Another political response paralleled the thinking that had been building throughout the French, British, and early American periods and emphasized the realization that Native Americans held interests separate from their alliance entanglements with Euro-American objectives—namely the preservation of their own land and way of life. The continuity of this realization from Nicolas and Pontiac in earlier eras now became focused by and on a Shawnee, Tecumseh, in the early nineteenth century.[18] He expressed the views he had delivered to Native Americans over a wide area of the eastern United States to Joseph Barron, Harrison's interpreter, in 1810:

> *The great spirit said he gave this great island to his red children. He placed the whites on the other side of the big water, they were not contented with their own, but came to take ours from us. They have driven us from the sea to the lakes, we can go no farther. They have taken upon themselves to say this tract belongs to the Miamis, this to the Delawares & so on. but the Great Spirit intended it as the common property of all the Tribes, nor can it be sold without the consent of all.*[19]

Espousing this philosophy, Tecumseh was in the process of developing a united front—a pan-Indian confederacy—among Native Americans north and south to confront the rapid loss of their resources. Treaty making halted after 1809 despite determined efforts from Harrison to acquire more cessions.

Tecumseh's brother Tenskwatawa (The Prophet) was a visionary who led another type of response—a nativistic revitalization movement.[20] Much as his predecessors in the eighteenth century, such as Wangomend or Neolin, Tenskwatawa's movement started as the result of a series of visionary experiences. He preached that a return to some of the old ways, the incorporation of his new ways, and a rejection of white ways (including material goods and alcohol) would lead to the deliverance of the Indian. He provided religious ceremonies and beliefs to Indian people at a time when personal and cultural disintegration was prevalent. In Indiana his influence was particularly strong among the Shawnee, Delaware, Potawatomi, and Kickapoo, and he attracted groups of Indians from as far away as Wisconsin to his Indiana base, Prophetstown, near present-day Lafayette. As a dynamic and charismatic religious leader, his message provided much of the impetus for his brother's political actions.

Pan-Indian movements cut across traditional tribal identity. They were also in conflict with the meager acculturation attempts of the Euro-Americans—a Moravian attempt at a mission on the White River among the Delaware (1801–06), a Quaker attempt to introduce European farming techniques to the Miami near Huntington (1806–07), and a more successful modern farming enterprise among the Delaware near Anderson (1809–12).[21] The

Moravians in particular came into conflict with the objectives of Tenskwatawa.

The pan-Indian political and religious adaptations helped bring on the War of 1812. The prelude to the war, the Battle of Tippecanoe, was the result of a Harrison-led expedition against Prophetstown. When war was officially declared, the initial American expeditions, such as that against the Miami Mississinewa villages in December 1812, focused on areas of resistance to Harrison's treaty progress. During the course of the war, at least twenty-five Indian villages and towns in Indiana were struck and destroyed. These included villages (and crops) of Miami, Potawatomi, Kickapoo, Winnebago, Delaware, Nanticoke, and Wyandot. Of the nineteen campaigns or engagements in Indiana, fifteen were initiated by U.S. troops or militia. Those initiated by the Indians included the sieges of Forts Wayne and Harrison, an attack of and near the Vallonia blockhouse, a fort in what is now Jackson County, Indiana, and the highly publicized Shawnee attack on the settlement at Pigeon Roost, near present-day Scottsburg, Indiana, in which twenty-three white men, women, and children were killed.[22]

The end of the war brought drastic changes for the tribes. Warfare was no longer a solution to the intrusion of ever-increasing numbers of Euro-Americans. Strong, experienced leaders such as Little Turtle (Miami), Pacanne (Miami), Blue Jacket (Shawnee), Five Medals (Potawatomi), and Tecumseh (Shawnee), died shortly before or during the War of 1812, making political changes necessary. The defeat of the British and twenty-five years of assaults on their economy had lessened the Indians' desire and resources to resist. Although the Miami (including the Eel River band), the Delaware, and the Potawatomi returned to their prewar locations in Indiana, the Piankashaw and the majority of the Wea and Kickapoo settled further west in Illinois and Missouri.

4

Statehood to Indian Removal, 1812–1840

Dear Sir, I want to get through law soon as practicable, for I long of
doing business for my Nation & for the Whites for their kindness to the
Native of the forest. I still remain your Most humble & obt. Servt.

Joseph N. Bourassa (Potawatomi student at Richard Johnson's
Choctaw Academy) to John Tipton, July 2, 1832

Burasa say he is going to study Law but I doubt it.

Richard Johnson to Thomas Henderson (Teacher at Choctaw),
January 10, 1835[1]

The Native Americans in Indiana faced different options after the War
of 1812 than prior to that conflict. Indian policies that had played one European power against another no longer worked; economically, many of their
resources had been destroyed during the war, leaving them destitute; and,
with Indiana becoming a state in 1816, the unrelenting incursions of white
settlers and their demand for land became constant. In addition, the pressures
that were to be exerted on them by the only government to which they had
recourse had already been expressed in 1803. President Thomas Jefferson,
having just acquired the Louisiana Territory, elaborated in a confidential letter
to William Henry Harrison, governor of Indiana Territory, on his vision for
Native Americans:

The decrease of game rendering their subsistence by hunting insufficient,
we wish to draw them to agriculture, to spinning and weaving. The latter
branches they take up with great readiness, because they fall to the women,
who gain by quitting the labours of the field [for] these which are exercised

within doors. When they withdraw themselves to the culture of a small
piece of land, they will perceive how useless to them are their extensive
forests, and will be willing to pare them off from time to time in exchange
for necessaries for their farms & families. To promote this disposition to
exchange lands which they have to spare and we want for necessaries, which
we have to spare and they want, we shall push our trading houses, and be
glad to see the good and influential individuals among them run in debt,
because we observe that when these debts get beyond what the individuals
can pay, they become willing to lop them off by a cession of lands. . . . In this
way our settlements will gradually circumscribe and approach the Indians,
and they will in time either incorporate with us as citizens of the United
States or remove beyond the Missisipi [sic].[2]

The territorial period was too chaotic to begin to implement what was
essentially an acculturate-or-remove policy, but after the War of 1812, this
generally held vision could be pursued. General Indian policy, however, was
not a state issue; it was the business ultimately of the federal government,
where Indian Affairs was lodged under the bureau of the Secretary of War with
direct supervision divided into regional agencies. As was the case during the
territorial period, the principal agency in Indiana in 1816 was initially located
at Fort Wayne and then moved to Logansport in 1828.

The Indian agent assigned to Fort Wayne in 1817 was Benjamin Stickney.
He was responsible for 1,400 Miami and Eel River Miami and 2,000 Potawatomi located in northeastern and north central Indiana. When asked for his
assessment of the civilizing program for Indians, Stickney was pessimistic for
several reasons. Driven by European trading policies, many Native Americans
had become addicted to alcohol and were unable to handle its effects. Besides
this "liquor problem," Stickney cited the Indian aversion to civilized habits,
dress, manners and customs; their attitude that European work habits were
akin to slavery; and the Indians' low esteem for the character of United States
citizens whom they perceived as principally driven by trade and speculation.[3]
He also provided interesting cultural descriptions of peoples who at that time
had been under some European influence for more than 150 years:

They have places that are commonly called villages, but perhaps not cor-
rectly, as they have no uniform place of residence. During the fall, winter,
and part of the spring, they are scattered in the woods, hunting. The
respective bands assemble in the spring at their several ordinary places of

*resort, where some have rude cabins made of small logs covered with bark;
but more commonly some poles stuck in the ground and tied together with
pliant slips of bark, and covered with large sheets of bark, or a kind of mat
made of flags. Near these places of resort they plant some corn. There are
eleven of these places of resort within my agency.*[4]

On religion and the Indians, Stickney observed: "They all believe in a God
as creator and governor, but have no idea of His will being communicated to
a man. . . . Their belief in a future existence is a kind of transubstantiation—a
removal from this existence to one more happy, with similar appetites and
enjoyments. They talk of a bad spirit, but never express any apprehensions of
his troubling them in their future existence."[5] In short, in Stickney's opinion,
the Native Americans of Indiana did not necessarily aspire to emulate what
had very rapidly become the majority population, nor were they very far along
the road in doing so.

What Stickney did not mention was that the Miami and Potawatomi
(about whom he was writing) were quite diverse by this point. How deeply
and successfully one was involved in the fur trade was always a differentiating
factor. Other factors were the number of descendants of intermarriages and
adopted captives now included in the tribes. Well known were William Wells
and Frances Slocum, whites who had been kidnapped and adopted into Indian
tribes as children, and their Miami families. By the time Stickney was writing,
Wells's Métis daughters had been educated in Kentucky, and his son was soon
to be a graduate of West Point. During this period Frances Slocum's birth family found her and took an active role in the well being of her and her children.
Also ignored were Métis fur traders who were to become part of the leadership
cadre, such as Francis and Lewis Godfroy and Jean Baptiste Richardville. All
the above were identified as Miami, and some would actively participate in
Miami affairs throughout this period. The Potawatomi were similarly diverse.
This heterogeneity meant that some would fare better than others during this
turbulent period following statehood.

Throughout this period the fur trade continued. In fact traders were
numerous, many Native Americans still pursued trapping as an occupation,
and trade goods were easily accessible and covered a wide range of conceivable
needs and desires. However, there were some not-so-subtle changes. As Jefferson had earlier suggested, the government's strategy was to encourage Indian
indebtedness so that the only way the debt could be eradicated was by the
cession of land. If one considers the option realistically, it is less "the fur trade"

A reckoning of accounts between the Ewing Brothers' trading firm and members of the Miami Nation in early December 1841 than, for the Indian, a way to coerce him from his land. The traders would "sell" or "trade" for whatever the Native American might want at usually rather steep prices. When the government called a treaty to alienate Indian lands, one of the treaty's provisions would be for the government to pay off the accumulated individual debts of a tribe. There then would be an investigation to ascertain the validity of each trader's claims, and if a claim was valid, the government would pay off the debt from the money given to the tribe for the cession. Each treaty also provided for cash annuities, and at annual distributions the money rapidly made its way from Indian to trader. Again trade goods were exchanged for something other than furs. In short, the "Indian business," an interaction between treaty, annuity, and land deals, was the primary economic enterprise in northern Indiana from 1818 to 1840, and the traders, in alliance with the federal Indian agent, were at the heart of it.

The circumstances of the traders themselves were quite varied. There were still many of the old-style French and Métis traders, but they were becoming outnumbered by the influx of American newcomers from the east. Many traders were agents of large trading outfits such as the American Fur Company (AFC). Others worked for smaller enterprises such as the Ewing Brothers' company, which survived competition with the larger AFC in northern Indiana and southern Michigan.[6] Among those traders who were independent or in varying partnerships were people who used the Indian trade as a stepping stone to later entrepreneurial endeavors. An example of the latter was Lathrop M. Taylor, who started as a clerk for a fur trading company in Fort Wayne in 1827 and had become a community leader and businessman in the pioneer village of South Bend by the time of the Indians' removal.[7] A somewhat different example is William Conner, whose Delaware wife and children were removed west with the Delaware while he remarried and "moved on."

During the early period of Indiana statehood, Native Americans were asked to make adjustments to their new circumstances. Federal officials launched a new wave of Indian policies as they resumed land acquisition treaties in 1818. The United States acquired large land cessions from the Miami, Delaware, and Potawatomi, followed shortly by similar cessions of their old claims by Piankashaw, Wea, and Kickapoo. These were not cessions of distant hunting and trapping grounds but came from the heart of Miami and Delaware occupation areas in central Indiana. With the new treaties came the first mention of an official removal policy. In 1818 the Delaware, some of whom had already moved from Indiana west of the Mississippi River, acquiesced to a removal clause and prepared for removal in 1820. Attached to these new treaties were individual allotments primarily given to Indian leaders (treaty signatories) and Métis tribal members. Ideally this plan was designed to reinforce the European rather than the Indian concept of land use, but in fact could also be interpreted as bribery. The bribery issue is given some currency by the fact that in the five Miami treaties from 1818 to 1840, Jean Baptist Richardville (principal chief and Métis) received 44¼ sections of land in allotments and Francis Godfroy (second "war" chief and Métis) 17 sections.[8] Another type of provision appeared, although minimally, in 1818: programs of acculturation began with granting the Miami two major agricultural resources, a gristmill and a sawmill.[9] In short, the policy communicated by Jefferson to Harrison in 1803 was now being implemented.

From 1818 through 1840 Indiana treaty negotiations followed each other in rapid succession. The effective land base in central Indiana of the Miami, Wea, Kickapoo, Delaware, and Wabash Potawatomi was ceded in the St. Mary's treaty of 1818 and the Fort Harrison treaty of 1819, which, with the exception of the Big Miami Reserve and some small reserves, relinquished all lands south of the Wabash River. In 1821 at Chicago, in 1828 at Carey Mission (near South Bend), and in 1832 at Tippecanoe, the Potawatomi, and in 1826 at Paradise Springs (Wabash), the Potawatomi and Miami ceded their effective land base north and west of the Wabash and Miami rivers, again with the exception of noncontiguous reserves.

Impetus was added to the overall land acquisition process by a series of events that came to be called the Black Hawk War. Black Hawk, a Sauk military leader from Illinois during the War of 1812, attempted to resettle a group of Indians from Iowa, where they had been removed, to Illinois in 1832, but the group was chased and eventually killed or imprisoned by American militia in Wisconsin. The event caused much panic among white settlers east of the Mississippi River, and in Indiana led to the removal of the peaceful and acculturated Vermillion Kickapoo and Potawatomi under Kenekuk, the Kickapoo Prophet, who lived at the mouth of Pipe Creek. Kenekuk was born near Lafayette and lived in that region to adulthood. As an adult he experienced a vision leading to an accommodationist form of revitalization movement. He and his people prospered in the rich bottom land as he preached docility even in the face of provocation, had the men do the farming, held weekly services using a prayer stick, and at the same time, carefully preserved important traditional cultural beliefs.[10] Despite the fact his small group's land had been alienated by

A Métis fur trader, Francis Godfroy became a leader among the Miami during the treaty and removal negotiations of the early nineteenth century.

LEWIS JAMES OTTO, THE ABORIGINAL PORT FOLIO, 1836.

treaty, he was still able to preserve the group in their traditional territory until 1832, when local and state demands for removal left them no recourse.

The largest remaining single Indian land holding, the Big Miami Reserve, comprising nearly 760,000 acres south of the Wabash River, was reduced in 1834. Land from this reserve would become Howard County and most of Cass, Clinton, Grant, Madison, Miami, Tipton, and Wabash counties. In the next two years the Potawatomi ceded their smaller reserves and agreed, although not unanimously, to remove. The forced removal of the Potawatomi, effected by the military and fittingly called the "Trail of Death," took place in 1838.[11] In 1838 and 1840, in the provisions of the last two Indiana treaties, the Miami ceded all but one small reserve and a number of individual allotments. They also agreed to remove with the provision that certain families be allowed to remain in Indiana. By 1840 the United States held all land previously owned by Native Americans in the state, with the exception of a single communally held reserve, Meshingomesia's, along the Mississinewa River in southern Wabash and northern Grant counties, and a scattering of individual allotments. All were held by Miami, the last Indian group in "the Land of Indians" to be removed.

Indian land loss occurred swiftly during the twenty-two-year period from 1818 to 1840. Out of the resistance of the Miami and Potawatomi to removal from their homeland, a strong political adaptation developed. Both the Miami and Potawatomi had a large population of Métis, many of whom were traders. The Métis acted as cultural intermediaries during the constant negotiations of the period. The astute leadership of, for example, Jean Baptiste Richardville, Francis Godfroy, and Metocinyah, a traditional leader, for the Miami delayed and frustrated the treaty and removal process. Leaders bought time and gained concessions that in the end permitted a number of Miami to avoid removal and remain in Indiana with some assets for survival. Earlier tacks of resistance were undercut by the American treaty process itself. The process of dealing tribe by tribe mitigated intertribal movements or pan-Indian spiritual renewal by constantly reinforcing tribal identity as the means to obtain benefits. It was not quite to the point of tribal enrollment leading to the tribal rolls found later in the century, but, by the end of this period, tribal annuities and other resources were increasingly handed out to individuals or family heads.

Despite delays, the process was unrelenting. In return for their land, the various tribes of Indiana received cash annuities, land allotments, gifts, salt, the elimination of debts claimed by traders, and desultory attempts to

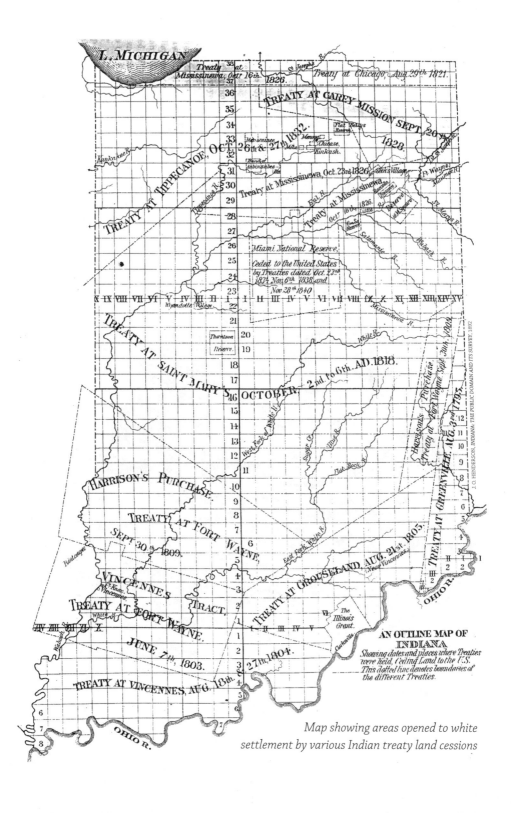

L. MICHIGAN

Treaty at Mississinewa, Oct. 16th 1826.

Treaty at Chicago, Aug. 29th 1821.

St. Joseph's

TREATY AT CAREY MISSION SEPT. 20th 1828

Flat Belays Reserve

Menomine Mota Menoqt Metea Chinese Kinkash

Thornd of Anbinatabee ville

Kankakee

TREATY AT TIPPECANOE, OCT. 26th & 27th 1832.

Tippecanoe R.

Treaty at Mississinewa, Oct. 23rd 1826.

Eel R.

Treaty at Mississinewa Oct. 16th 1826.

Little R.
Reserve
Rom.Sc. Reserve
Salamonie

Beek's Village
Reserve
F. Wayne
Miamia R.
St. Marys R.
Wabash R.

Miami National Reserve,

Ceded to the United States by Treaties dated Oct. 23rd 1834, Nov. 6th 1838, and Nov. 28th 1840

Mississinewa R.

X IX VIII VII VI V IV III II I — I II III IV V VI VII VIII IX X XI XII XIII XIV XV

Wyandotte Village

TREATY AT SAINT MARY'S OCTOBER 2nd to 6th A.D. 1818.

Thorntown Reserve

White R.

Harrison's Purchase, Treaty at Fort Wayne Sept. 30th 1809.

Treaty at Greenville Aug. 3rd 1795.

J. O. HENDERSON, INDIANA: THE PUBLIC DOMAIN AND ITS SURVEY, 1892.

West Fork of White R.

Sugar Cr.

Blue R.

Flat Rock

HARRISON'S PURCHASE.

TREATY AT FORT WAYNE, SEPT. 30th 1809.

East Fork White R.

TREATY AT GROUSELAND, AUG. 21st 1805. Near Vincennes

Kankakee

VINCENNES'S

Ft. Knox Vincennes

TREATY AT FORT WAYNE.

TRACT.

White R.

Wabash R.

JUNE 7th, 1803.

& 27th, 1804.

TREATY AT VINCENNES, AUG. 18th & 27th 1804.

The Illinois Grant.

Charlotte

OHIO

AN OUTLINE MAP OF
INDIANA

Showing dates and places where Treaties were held, Ceding Land to the U.S. This dotted line denotes boundaries of the different Treaties.

OHIO R.

Map showing areas opened to white settlement by various Indian treaty land cessions

Jean Baptiste Richardville was the principal Miami chief from 1816 to his death in 1841. During the post-War-of-1812-treaty period he was successful in delaying and ameliorating Miami removal from Indiana.

acculturate them to a new way of life. At the top of that acculturation list was the goal to make farmers out of Indian males. Allotments were in part an attempt to impart pride in individual ownership in a people who valued a communal way of living. Other treaty stipulations included funds for fencing and clearing land; agricultural implements and wagons; domesticated animals, including yokes of oxen; mills, both grist and saw; teachers of agricultural and domestic arts; and blacksmiths. There were also general funds for education for both the Potawatomi and Miami.

Education was to be the capstone of acculturation. Prior to this period between statehood and removal, Métis children of individuals such as William Burnett, William Wells, and Jean Baptiste Richardville were sent to Detroit or Kentucky for an education. Now was deemed the right time to embark on a broader approach. The two prime movers of this approach were Colonel Richard M. Johnson and Reverend Isaac McCoy, both Baptists who came out of the revival movement in Kentucky in the early nineteenth century. Beyond those similarities, these were two very different men. Johnson was a veteran of the War of 1812 and credited by some with killing Tecumseh at the Battle of the Thames.[12] He then served in Congress and was vice president of the United States under Martin Van Buren. While in Congress he introduced a Baptist Convention petition dealing with an appropriation for the civilization of the Indians in 1819 and then founded Choctaw Academy at his home at Great Crossings, Kentucky, in 1825.[13] Choctaw was opened to Indiana Miami and Potawatomi students from 1826 to 1841.

McCoy was a Baptist missionary who ran schools near Vincennes (1819–20), Fort Wayne (1820–22), and Carey Mission (1822–30). McCoy's ambition was to organize an Indian state in the West and, one imagines, to have an important role in its administration.[14] He was clearly in step with the government's removal plans. John Tipton, Indian agent at Fort Wayne and then Logansport, was very interested in the potential of education and directed funding to the institutions of Johnson and McCoy for Miami and Potawatomi students under his jurisdiction. Approximately 125 Potawatomi and 25 Miami were exposed to formal education during this period. The duration of time "in school" ranged from less than one to ten years.[15]

Education for these students shared much in common with the white structure of the time in educational techniques, curriculum, texts, and skills training. In the late 1820s Johnson experimented with the Lancastrian method, an inexpensive system for organizing effective schools that featured strict discipline and order and that was becoming popular in large American cities. Johnson's Lancastrian school was directed by teacher, Thomas Henderson, with the help of tutors. One notable Indian tutor was the Potawatomi Joseph N. Bourassa. Choctaw Academy in particular foreshadowed the Indian boarding school systems found later in the century. Choctaw was all male and culturally heterogeneous since it was originally directed to, as its name implies, students from the southeast. The rigid approach to education continued as the school added, among others, Miami and Potawatomi from Indiana in 1826. Choctaw assigned the students English names on arrival (for example, George Washington, Lewis Cass, Thomas Jefferson), except for Métis children who already had European names. Students dressed uniformly at Choctaw and boarded there, as they came from some distance. Although Carey Mission was probably designed along the same lines, it was apparently less rigorous, partially perhaps because it was coeducational and the students were primarily Potawatomi from nearby areas. Dress varied, and naming was less an issue.[16]

These attempts at acculturation leading to assimilation were applied to people who were in the midst of losing both the land and the way of life they valued. Their ancestors had gradually adapted to the fur trade system, and it was this way of life combined with the evolution of their own cultures that they had to relinquish or else leave the lands they and their ancestors had occupied for generations. For this they were given trinkets, relief for debt that they were manipulated to incur, small pieces of land meant for individual farms, tools for men to do women's work and women's roles that devalued their contributions, opportunities not sought to become individual farmers or to be educated in white schools, and, of course, money. Those who were given the "capstone" opportunity of education often found that the experience created in them ambitions that the American people would never let them fulfill, while at the same time, they lost touch with their own roots. In 1838 John Tipton, now a U.S. senator, gave his assessment of the educational experiment he had long supported:

Scarcely had the work of improvement commenced before it was destroyed by the rapid influx of white population, and it all ended in disappointment. . . . I had frequent opportunities to visit the school conducted by the society (Baptist Missionary), and it is but an act of justice to bear testimony to the prudence, economy, and industry with which it was conducted, and I

*had the mortification to witness its failure, from the causes which I
have stated.*[17]

Although speaking to the education program, Tipton put his finger on the
basic problem for the Native Americans in Indiana during this era—the rapid
influx of white settlers, which allowed no time for adaptation or acculturation.

The most numerous targets of the misapplied and often unscrupulous
treaty process and, ultimately, removal between 1818 and 1840 were the
Delaware, Potawatomi, and Miami (including the Eel River), who probably
numbered, at the beginning of the period, fewer than 4,000 individuals. In
1824, after the removal of the Delaware and other remnant groups, such as
the remainder of the Wea, Tipton listed the number of Potawatomi, Miami,
and Eel River under his supervision as 1,368, 848, and 225, respectively—a
total of 2,441 individuals.[18]

After two hundred years of contact with Euro-Americans, the Native
American population experienced rapid and disruptive cultural change. Many
of the earlier changes were voluntary to accommodate participation in the fur
trade. Changes that occurred during the period following the War of 1812,
however, were forced by both swiftly deteriorating conditions and the manipulation of white officials and speculators. It was from this period that the most
dense record of the region's Native Americans can be found. There were also
purposeful attempts to record their culture as such. Most notable examples
of the latter are Charles C. Trowbridge's descriptions of the Miami and Shawnee and George Winter's paintings of the Miami and Potawatomi.[19] Although
limited to one primary informant and exploration of few topics, Trowbridge's
report on the Miami confirms the continuing importance of both the Midewiwin and traditional political practices. Winter's paintings reveal visible
culture and demonstrate the culmination of the unique style of Miami and
Potawatomi appearance derived from their long participation in the fur trade.

The depictions of this period record the way of life of peoples who were
considered to be disappearing. It was perceived that extinction, assimilation,
or removal had been or were to be the fate of all of Indiana's Indians. The
Mascouten were extinct, and assimilation programs were underway for all
eastern Native Americans. Forced or self-removal had already effected the
westerly movement of the majority of the Piankashaw and Wea, the Delaware
and Nanticoke, the Kickapoo, Shawnee, and Potawatomi, leaving only the
Miami as an intact tribe wholly within Indiana by 1840.

5

After Indian Removal, 1840–1870

Me shin go me zia Did not come here to sell his land. . . . He wants [it] for his women and young men, & children now growing up.

Minutes of a conference with Miami delegation, Washington, DC, May 23–June 5, 1854, regarding ratified treaty no. 274[1]

By the late 1840s only a remnant of the former Indian population of Indiana remained in the state. Officially, there should have been no Indians left in the state, as the removal legislation signed by President Andrew Jackson in 1830 clearly called for moving all Indians from east of the Mississippi River to territories west of the river. Altogether, more than 100,000 Indian people from twenty-three tribes were moved from eastern states between 1830 and 1850. The legislation permitted choice, but when Menominee, a village chief in northwest Indiana, clearly chose to stay, he was jailed and his Potawatomi villagers were marched west. Many other Indians moved to more western areas before Indian removal was made official policy. Whether driven by humanitarian concerns or greed for land—or both—the purpose of Indian removal legislation was ethnic cleansing, taking away the remainder of a specific ethnic population, Indians, from where they had lived for generations. Ethnic cleansing through removal was not genocide, though many died in the process.[2]

Indian removal, while thorough, was not total. Some Indian people quietly hid out and remained in Indiana, avoiding the occasional efforts to collect "skulkers" and send them west. Others who were removed literally walked back to Indiana and took refuge among those who were permitted to remain. Some people of mixed Indian and white heritage chose assimilation, leaving behind Indian ethnicity for identity as Americans. Records were not kept of the non-tribal Indians who stayed behind. They were not counted on U.S. censuses and most often became a hidden people. Their family's Indian ethnicity or identity was only expressed generations later when prejudice against Indians lessened. While Indians not recognized as such may have constituted a far larger number than tribal Indians, there is very little documentation of their lives. For this reason, it is necessary to begin with the histories of the tribal Indians of Indiana.

The Potawatomi of Michigan and Indiana were granted exemption from removal in a treaty they signed in Chicago in 1833. Located in the South Bend area and in neighboring southwestern Michigan, this small band of Indians frustrated federal removal policy and began its modern history in the Michiana region. Leopold Pokagon, the leader of this small, Catholic Potawatomi tribe, forcefully argued that his people were already moving toward individual ownership of land and there was no need to force them from land that was not a commonly held reservation.[3] On that basis, the treaty commissioners at Chicago relented and allowed them to remain on their lands. In 1837, the year Michigan became a state and as the South Bend area became heavily settled, Pokagon began purchasing land around Silver Lake, some twenty miles north of South Bend near today's Dowagiac, Michigan. Within a year or so he had bought 874 acres, all from the public land office in Kalamazoo. Pokagon's people all settled at Silver Lake within two years.[4]

Though allowed by treaty to remain in Michigan, confusion over Catholic Potawatomi status led to continued pressure for their removal. In 1840 the secretary of war ordered the commanding general based at Detroit to remove all remaining Potawatomi from Michigan and northern Indiana. Pokagon, however, was not about to allow the treaty rights he had fought for to be broken by ignorance of the 1833 treaty or misunderstanding on the part of the U.S. government. With fellow leaders he traveled to Detroit and met with an associate justice of the Michigan Supreme Court, Epaphroditus Ransom. Ransom wrote a legal opinion based on the 1833 treaty emphasizing the exempt status of Pokagon's group. Ransom further stated that if the group were gathered for removal, he would free them with a writ of habeas corpus. In short, no federal authority, including the U.S. army, had the right to force them west. In what happened to be the last year of his life, Pokagon obtained a clear and final recognition of the legal status of the Catholic Potawatomi to stay in Michigan.[5]

After Pokagon's death in 1840, one of his sons named Peter was joined by other village leaders to guide the tribe. They were assisted by a German

Chief Leopold Pokagon, who led a small group of Catholic Potawatomi near South Bend and in southwest Michigan

missionary, Brother Joseph (Charles Rother), who was an experienced farmer. He helped the group create small farmsteads. For three days a week, they worked together building homes, clearing and fencing fields, and putting in crops. On other days, the men would hunt and cut firewood. Apparently the Potawatomi men were able to overcome the woodland Indian belief that farming was women's work. By 1850 people began moving away from the Pokagon reserve at Silver Creek to Rush Lake and Brush Creek, further north in Van Buren County, Michigan, and roughly fifteen miles west of the older community at Paw Paw. Over the next fourteen years these four communities defined the Potawatomi settlement.[6]

The Potawatomi continued to acculturate—that is, to adapt to some American ways of doing things while retaining their Indian identity. During the 1850s and 1860s men began doing more seasonal work in agriculture and semi-skilled work in local industries and trades. However, they also continued more traditional activities such as hunting, fishing, and gathering wild foods and medicinal plants.[7] For many years, American officials had encouraged assimilation as policy, hoping that Indians would give up their culture and merge into American society. By the 1840s that policy had already failed in the face of general American Indian determination to maintain tribal identity and ways of life.

One political issue remained important to the Catholic Potawatomi. They were still owed annuities—money guaranteed by their treaties—that were not paid in the 1830s and 1840s. Showing adaptation to American ways, leaders lobbied the federal government. In 1864 a leader named Singowa headed a delegation that traveled to Washington, DC, to present the issue of money owed to the tribe. A year later, the Senate Committee of Indian Affairs confirmed that the Catholic Potawatomi should, indeed, be paid for the missing annuities. The Senate report also noted that the Indians were citizens of Michigan "and yet members of a tribe with special rights of their own."[8]

Partial success on the annuity issue came on July 28, 1866, when Congress passed a joint resolution awarding $39,000 to the tribe. A special agent was appointed to distribute the payment among all tribal members. An important provision of the settlement was that this would be a final payment to the tribe. This "final payment" clause brought a storm of protest from leaders who felt they were due annuities after 1833 as well. Special agent William Corkhill paid $169.50 in gold and silver coins to each Indian. A new tribal roll was made listing name, gender, age, and family membership for a total of 230 people. The Potawatomi showed that they understood the modern meaning of

money, making improvements on their homes and farms, paying on mortgages, and generally improving their economic positions.[9]

In some ways, the experience of the Miami Indians of Indiana paralleled
that of the Potawatomi of Michigan and Indiana. In other ways, however,
the Indiana Miami were quite different in their tribal culture and levels of
acculturation and style of leadership. As with the Potawatomi, the removal
period and the years following were important in shaping the future of the
Miami people.

The history of the Indiana Miami tribe began on October 6, 1846, with the
removal of 323 Miami from Peru, Indiana, to Kansas Territory. Provisions of
the Miami treaties of 1838 and 1840 allowed 126 Miami to remain in Indiana.
Forty-three of this group belonged to the family of John Baptiste Richardville, the mixed-blood principal chief of the Miami who died at Fort Wayne in
1841. Twenty-eight more belonged to the family of Francis Godfroy, another
prominent mixed-blood chief who died near Peru in 1840. The remaining 55
belonged to the family of Metocinyah, a Miami chief who died along the
Mississinewa River in today's Grant County in 1832. In 1845 Congress passed
a resolution permitting the descendants of Frances Slocum, the elderly white
captive, and her Miami husband Shapoconah (Deaf Man) to stay in Indiana,
adding another 22 to the tribe. This small group, totaling 148, was the nucleus
of today's Miami Nation of Indiana.[10]

Very shortly after removal two more groups were allowed to stay with the
Miami. In 1847 the Eel River Miami, culturally related to the Miami but politically distinct, sued against removal. A local judge freed the Indians on a writ
of habeas corpus, and the 17 women and children took refuge with the Miami
near Peru.[11] Mazequah, one of the chiefs taken west, returned to Indiana with
his two wives, nephew, and brother-in-law. On May 1, 1850, Congress passed
a joint resolution allowing Mazequah and his extended family as well as several other Miami who had treaty reserves to remain in Indiana, adding another
101 people to the Indiana group. About 60 of the Kansas returnees took
refuge on the Godfroy treaty reserve east of Peru.[12] There were now six groups
or extended families of Miami in Indiana. They varied greatly in adaptation
to American society. The Catholic Miami were perhaps the most acculturated,
while the followers of Meshingomesia (Metocinyah's son) were probably the
least acculturated. The other groups fell somewhere in between.

By 1850 a majority of the Miami Indians of Indiana had defeated federal
removal policy if one judges by the number of Indians residing in Kansas and
Indiana. At that time the Kansas tribe had about 100 members, while 250

resided in Indiana.[13] Most of those in Indiana lived on some fifteen thousand acres of land remaining from treaty reserves, most of them in Miami, Wabash, Grant, and Allen counties.[14] The treaty reserves chosen for Miami residence were all located on rivers where Miami people could continue their annual subsistence cycle of hunting, fishing, fowling, horticulture, and gathering edible and medicinal plants. While game animals had grown scarce, the rivers still abounded in fish, and river bottomlands contained a variety of soil types supporting many kinds of edible plants and fruit-bearing shrubs and trees. The Miami lands between Peru, Marion, and Wabash were connected by a series of trails and paths, making for easy communication by horse or by foot. Very little ancient forest had been cleared, and large areas of wetland remained in river bottomlands.[15]

Nearly all Miami marriages during the first generation after removal were by Indian custom, conducted by tribal leaders and not recorded in Indiana civil records. The old custom of plural marriages continued among some tribal leaders. When William Godfroy sold a parcel of land in 1868, the Miami County recorder duly requested the "X" marks of both wives on the deed.[16] The most important rule of marriage was the prohibition against marrying within a tribal group. Marrying outside one's group was strictly observed in marriages between Miami individuals throughout the nineteenth century.[17] Marriages between the six groups of Miami created strong ties of kinship throughout the tribe. At the same time, each group was led by a chief or tribal council member and had its own identity as the "Meshingomesia Miami," "Richardville Miami," and so on. Indian-style divorce remained common as well, meaning that a dissatisfied husband or wife would simply walk out of a marriage.[18]

At death Miami were buried on tribal land, often near the home of a leader. In the nineteenth century, deaths were rarely recorded in county records, and the Miami buried their own. In testimony given in 1872, Pecongeoh (Charles Peconga), a son of Meshingomesia, described Miami burial customs:

> When a person dies, they go and bury him, but still they say his spirit is there at the house yet. They say that when they don't make an adoption, the spirit still stays there and all the rest of the family keep dying off. . . . The one that is adopted does not take the place of the one that died—it is in order to get the spirit of the one that is dead to Heaven, the same thing that you would call a funeral.[19]

Usually favorite objects of the deceased were placed in or on the grave. Years later Sarah Wadsworth recalled seeing the burial of Francis Wildcat (Peshewa) in 1855 when she was a girl living in Miami County. She stated that the assembled group ate and then placed food near the head of the deceased. Wildcat's favorite horse was killed for his journey to the spirit land.[20]

Measured changes came to the Miami community in the 1850s and 1860s. Meshingomesia, Peter Bondy, and Pimyotamah converted to the Baptist church. Bondy, born about 1817, was married to Frances Slocum's younger daughter Ozahshinquah; Pimyotamah, born about 1818, was a son-in-law of Francis Godfroy. Meshingomesia allowed a Baptist church and a one-room school to be built near his house on the reservation to encourage the adoption of American ways. Wahcaconah, another resident on the Meshingomesia reservation, also built a Baptist church. For many years, Pimyotamah's house was used for Baptist church services as well. Land was slowly cleared, and log houses and outbuildings were built by white sharecroppers under contract to the Indians.[21]

Annuities from earlier treaties provided each Miami person with fifteen to twenty dollars a year in cash, allowing for the purchase of everyday items at local general stores. The Miami had been buying manufactured clothing, tools, and utensils for generations. Daybooks of the Adam Parker store at La Fontaine, Indiana, near the Meshingomesia reservation show purchases of sugar, coffee, spices, and other food items as well as eating utensils, shoes and clothing, and a variety of garden tools.[22] The everyday items used by the Miami were very similar to those used by rural whites, even as Miami values and beliefs remained very different.

One of the fundamental distinctions of the Miami from other ethnic groups in Indiana was political. The Miami allowed to remain in the state were exempted from removal by federal Indian law. Their treaty land grants could not be sold without permission of the president of the United States. Treaty land was also exempt from state taxation. The Miami were not U.S. citizens or citizens of the state of Indiana, and they could not become citizens without congressional legislation. They were not allowed to vote and most often were not counted on the U.S. census. At the same time, the federal government did not want to recognize their tribal government, insisting that the Miami government was in Kansas and that all legal issues the Indiana Miami had should be dealt with by leaders in Kansas.[23]

Meshingomesia led the Miami who remained in Indiana after removal of a portion of the tribe to Kansas Territory in 1846.

The Miami leaders in Indiana were experienced in tribal government and realized they were vulnerable to manipulation if their tribal government was not recognized by the United States. After removal, Meshingomesia was chosen to lead the Miami. Born about 1800, he was the oldest leader of the extended family groups. He was also responsible for a 5,500-acre reservation held in common by all the members of his group. He was long noted for his prudent leadership of the largest group within the tribe. Meshingomesia was joined by Bondy and Pimyotamah. Thomas Richardville, a grandson of Chief Jean Baptiste Richardville who was born about 1830, was the leader of the Fort Wayne Miami. He, too, had converted to the Baptist faith. In about 1860 he moved to Kansas. While he returned to Indiana from time to time and sometimes advised the Indiana tribal council, he was never a member. These Indiana Miami leaders began shortly after removal to assert their separate tribal status from the Miami in Kansas.[24]

In 1854 George Manypenny, the commissioner of Indian affairs, called Kansas and Indiana Miami leaders to Washington, DC, to negotiate changes in earlier treaties. When the Indiana delegation arrived in Washington in late May, Manypenny immediately pressured Meshingomesia to sell the reservation. Meshingomesia declined, saying the land was for "his women and young men, & children now growing up." When the sale of land was brought up again, Meshingomesia sat silent, the Indian way of saying, "Absolutely not!"[25] Another issue for the Indiana leadership was purging unwanted Miami individuals from the tribal roll. In 1851 Congress had bypassed the Indiana tribal government and added sixty-eight distant relatives of Chief Richardville to annuity rolls along with the followers of Papakeechi (Flat Belly), a Miami leader who had moved in with the Potawatomi of Michigan and Indiana. Neither the Richardville relatives nor Papakeechi's band had lived among the Indiana Miami or participated in their community. While the Miami leaders were in Washington, they insisted that the right to determine tribal membership was theirs.[26]

When the treaty was signed on June 5, 1854, the Miami delegation had achieved its goals. Payment of annuities was to be only to people on the list of tribal members approved by the tribal council. The original annuities due to the tribe would be ended, but the commissioner set up a trust fund of $231,000. Interest on this fund would pay the tribe annuities until 1881, when the trust fund would be divided equally among tribal members. Finally, and most important of all, Manypenny recognized the Miami of Indiana as having "a fully authorized deputation" that would negotiate separately from the Kansas Miami with representatives of the U.S. Senate. Written into the treaty, this meant the U.S. government recognized the Miami tribal government as the representative of the Miami of Indiana separate from the Kansas tribal government. The U.S. Senate ratified the treaty on August 4, 1854.[27]

However, the ink was hardly dry on the treaty before it was broken. In 1858 Congress added more "Miamis at large" to the tribal membership. Today we might refer to these non-tribal Miami as ethnic Indians. Though of Miami heritage, the added people were not among the 278 persons the tribal council had accepted in the tribal roll (list of membership) made in accordance with the 1854 treaty. The tribal council protested immediately, writing the Indian commissioner that "we protest, consent not, and allow not, the Pottawatomies and others to share with us the Interest of our Annuities. It is contrary to our treaty . . . that no other persons shall be added to the payroll list without the consent of the Miami Tribe of Indians of Indiana."[28] Congress added more people in 1862, increasing the illegal tribal members to 119 people. Over sixteen years, this group diverted about one third of the income from the Miami trust fund.[29]

In 1867 the Miami of Indiana found able attorneys and achieved affirmation of their treaty rights. Congress then passed legislation confirming the right of the tribe to control its membership and cut the "bogus Miami" from tribal rolls. Most important of all, Henry Stanbery, the U.S. Attorney General, ruled that the "rights of these persons are fixed, not merely on the footing of law, but of solemn contract, and should not be changed or disturbed except by their consent."[30] When Indiana attempted to tax Miami treaty reserves in the late 1860s, the commissioner of Indian affairs ruled that so long as the tribal government was recognized by the federal government, "their property is withdrawn from the operation of state laws."[31]

By 1870 the Potawatomi of Michigan and Indiana and the Indiana Miami had achieved legal status as tribes behind the frontier. With capable leadership, both tribes had openly confronted the wishes of the federal government to take them west and had asserted treaty rights protecting them in their homeland. The similarity of achievement, however, masked differences between the two communities. The Catholic Potawatomi had adapted more consistently to American life, including owning private property and having an elective government based on American models of local government. They were citizens of Michigan as well as tribal citizens. With a population of similar size to the Miami, the Potawatomi were far more dispersed among the white population, which furthered adaptation to everyday American life.

In contrast to the Catholic Potawatomi, the Miami retained an older form of consensus government led by hereditary leaders. While some portions of the tribe were highly acculturated, the majority lived between the Wabash and Mississinewa rivers east of Peru on treaty grants or the Meshingomesia reservation, often spoke the Miami language in daily life, and kept up many subsistence activities while relying on annuities for purchase of everyday goods. Under these circumstances, adaptation was slower and more uneven. The fact that they were not citizens and their land was not taxed left them vulnerable to non-Indian efforts to deprive them of the legal status to gain access to their resources.

6

Tribalism Endangered, 1870–1900

My people, the Miamis, made peace with the whites in Washington's time and we never violated it. . . . The red men made their treaties and kept them, but the white men did not.

Gabriel Godfroy, speech at Tippecanoe Battlefield site, June 16, 1907[1]

In 1870 the Miami of Indiana and the Potawatomi of Michigan and Indiana had seasoned leaders and a sense of confidence about their place in American society. Unlike western tribes falling under the control of the reservation system with Indian agents and Indian police to force assimilation, the Miami and Potawatomi were adapting to change by choice. They were defining what it was to be Indian behind the frontier. Both tribes had grievances concerning money they believed they were owed by the federal government. This issue called for the tribal governments to make decisions, hire attorneys, and to act decisively to protect tribal rights.

The next thirty years were to be critical to the future of both tribes. In the language of ethnic studies, adaptation of cultures to new ways while preserving distinctive values is called acculturation. Acculturation can bring great change, but it is usually change by choice. American officials and those anxious to develop the Great Plains were growing weary of the pace and uneven nature of Indian acculturation. After the Civil War, the U.S. government was more anxious than ever to solve the "Indian Problem," the "problem" being the desire of Indians to keep their land, their treaty rights, and their cultures—in other words, their very identity as Indians. In order to begin a new form of ethnic cleansing based on purging Indians of their "Indianness," Congress ended the making of treaties in 1871 and took direct control of Indian affairs.

The tools for forced assimilation included the now familiar missionary efforts to make Christians of Indians. They also included two new strategies, boarding schools for children and dividing or allotting the commonly held land of reservations into private landholdings for individuals. Once Indians had been culturally transformed into Americans and established on their individually owned plots of land, they would receive American citizenship, and treaty rights would end. Tribal governments would be eliminated, as there would no longer be a need for them. Indians, of course, resisted these heavy-handed and destructive measures to erase their culture and rights.

The Potawatomi of Michigan and Indiana had already made many adaptations to American life. Tribal land was privately held rather than commonly owned. Some Indian men were farming American style and had settled on individual plots of land. The three hundred or so members of the tribe were scattered from Hartford, Michigan, in the north to Benton Harbor on Lake Michigan, east as far as Cassopolis, and south of the Indiana state line. The dispersion of tribal members increased as people sought jobs as casual workers or in towns and cities.[2]

Family and social changes occurred as well. In the 1840s traditional clan names were used, but by 1866 clan names had often become last names. Women began to take on their husband's last names as their own. Many older clan names showing a connection with bears, fish, or other creatures tended to fall out of use.[3] Hunting, fishing, and gathering remained important activities, but increasing job opportunities in the rapidly growing area of southwest Michigan drew people into wage work as well as farming. Prevalent membership in the Catholic Church encouraged acculturation as well.

The conclusion drawn by local non-Indians was that the "final payment" of 1866 was the end of the Potawatomi tribal organization. A local historian said that with the 1866 payment, "the reason for the tribal organization [among the Catholic Potawatomi] ceased to exist and the Indians were placed on the same basis as other citizens."[4] It was assumed that there was no further reason for the existence of a tribal government. Whites expected that the members of the tribe would simply blend (assimilate) into the general population. Potawatomi leaders, however, interpreted the 1866 "final payment" very differently. They believed the payment was merely a partial settlement of unpaid annuities. Being made to sign off on what American officials insisted was a final payment greatly reinforced their sense of injustice while showing that if they worked together, they could continue as an Indian tribe.

The first thing the Catholic Potawatomi did was to completely reorganize their political system, moving away from traditional informal governance by consensus decisions of hereditary leaders to the American system of formal governance. The tribe adopted a new name as "Potawatomi of Michigan and Indiana" and began nominating and electing their officers at public meetings. Officers were a principal chief, a chairman of the business committee, a secretary, and seven business committeemen. The business committee served as

SIMON POKAGON, O-GÎ-MÂW-KWE MIT-Î-GWÂ-KÎ (QUEEN OF THE WOODS), 1899

Simon Pokagon (1830–1899), who attended the University of Notre Dame (Indiana) and Oberlin College (Ohio), was a Chautauqua speaker and pressed for settlement of treaty claims (James Clifton, The Prairie People, 1977).

the executive branch, conducting daily business and meeting the tribal membership twice or more each year. Committee members represented the older village communities such as Paw Paw. Because the community was scattered over a large area, meetings were rotated to Dowagiac, Hartford, or Watervliet or to the farms of more prosperous leaders. The tribal government had effectively adapted Michigan's system of township government to tribal needs.[5]

By 1869 the tribe was working again to contest the U.S. position that they had received their final payment for claims on annuities. Attorney William Severance was hired to lobby the tribe's claim in Washington, DC. After the Civil War and the end of treaty making, Congress had to pass legislation to enable a tribe to proceed with claims. For tribes, getting legislation passed was a difficult job at best. By 1872, however, Severance had persuaded the House and Senate Committees on Indian Affairs to report on the tribal complaint. The Senate committee agreed that the "final annuity" clause of the 1866 agreement was fraudulent and that the tribe was owed substantial annuities. The information gathered allowed the claim to move forward.[6]

In 1882 Severance was replaced as tribal attorney by John Critcher, a member of a powerful Chicago firm with offices in Washington, DC. A year later, the commissioner of Indian affairs and the secretary of the interior certified that the organization called the "Potawatomi of Michigan and Indiana" was a tribal government recognized by the United States and approved Critcher's contract to work for the tribe. Soon after, various other groups of Potawatomi, either tribal members or individuals, asserted that they were connected with the tribe. Finally, in January 1890 Congress passed the necessary legislation permitting the tribe to sue the United States in the Court of Claims, twenty-one years after the claim was first presented.[7]

At this point, many non-tribal or "hidden" Indians came forth in an attempt to get some part of the award. By 1890 thousands of such people were scattered throughout the Midwest, but especially in Ontario, the Upper Peninsula of Michigan, Indiana, Iowa, Wisconsin, and Minnesota. It is important to state that these people were of Indian descent and years or generations ago had been connected with various Potawatomi groups and sometimes granted land or annuities. They often identified as Indian but were not tribal. Today they would be called ethnic Indians. Later treaties or tribal governments had for various reasons removed them from tribal membership. Thus their Indian identity was personal, not defined by law. The issue for the

Potawatomi of Michigan and Indiana was not whether they were "Indian" but whether they were legally members of the tribe.[8]

The case was decided once the U.S. Court of Claims had examined in careful detail an enormous body of evidence gathered from 1843 onward. Included were all the congressional investigations, court records and decisions, and specific annuity payments made over the years. The easiest issue for the court to decide was the amount of the award. It came to $104,626 for unpaid back annuities, plus interest that would accrue until the money was paid out.[9] The U.S. Supreme Court ruled that the commissioner of Indian affairs should decide the thorny question of who should share in the award.

In the summer of 1895, a special agent, John W. Cadman, began working to create a tribal roll. After the agent's sudden death, Marcus D. Shelby was appointed and finished the work in March 1896. The Cadman-Shelby roll contained 273 names, all of them approved by the tribal government and all people well known over a long period of time as tribal members.[10] Several prominent persons, especially from the South Bend area, were rejected because they had never participated directly in the tribe. Many of these individuals had a Potawatomi ancestor or had once drawn annuities, but they had not identified for many years as Potawatomi. Perhaps they were ethnic Indians but did not meet criteria to share tribal funds. In terms of future distinctions between ethnic and tribal Catholic Potawatomi, the Cadman-Shelby roll of 1896 became critical.[11]

While the Potawatomi of Michigan and Indiana faced one major issue in the 1870s, the Indiana Miami faced several challenges. Land issues were first and foremost. In November 1867 the aging Meshingomesia wrote the commissioner of Indian Affairs asking that the communal reservation owned by the members of his extended family be divided into private land for each person. It is not known how much influence white advisors had in this petition.[12] In general, judging by the outcome for the Miami, the pressure to privatize the reservation may have been considerable.

In 1872 Congress passed legislation for allotment of the Meshingomesia reservation into "farms" for eligible Miami.[13] From May 14 to July 7, 1873, testimony was taken from many Miami at the schoolhouse on the reservation to ascertain who had a right to share in the land. Most of the testimony was in the Miami language. Thomas Richardville and two of Meshingomesia's grandsons who were bilingual acted as interpreters. Nearly all names were given in

Indiana Miami leader Gabriel Godfroy, son of Francis Godfroy, with Gabriel's youngest son George Durand Godfroy. The photo was taken at Gabriel's home in Butler Township, Miami County, Indiana, ca. 1903. Gabriel is wearing the Frances Slocum blanket. Through work with Gabriel Godfroy, Jacob Piatt Dunn preserved much of the Miami language. Durand Godfroy died in 1940.

the Miami language, and Miami kinship terminology was used. The interviews indicate that the members of the Meshingomesia group were the least acculturated Miami. The resulting several hundred pages of carefully hand-written testimony offer firsthand commentary by dozens of Miami people on family life, beliefs, customs, and attitudes and are an invaluable snapshot of tribal culture.[14]

The three commissioners appointed to take the testimony ascertained that sixty-three members of Meshingomesia's band of Miami were eligible for land. Surveyors were sent to divide the land into allotments that were equal in value. It was found that the reservation encompassed 5,468 acres. The individual allotments or "headrights" varied from 77 to 125 acres depending on the quality of the soil and the lay of the land for agriculture.[15] Congress exempted the allotments from taxes, mortgages, and sale until January 7, 1881. On that date the sixty-three Miami would become U.S. citizens and were free to dispose of their land if they wished.[16]

Various problems plagued the new Miami landowners from the beginning. Women still far outnumbered men in the tribe. Thirty-seven of the allottees were female; twenty-six were male. Just before the transition to private ownership, tuberculosis swept through the local Miami community. A majority of the men old enough to potentially manage land died. All of the property holders under age twenty-one had white guardians. In 1881 each Miami person received a $695 payment when the trust fund from the 1854 treaty was divided. While this money was a benefit to many, all minor children were required by law to have a white guardian. Guardians tended to overcharge their young clients and in some cases to take over their assets. When the Indians became adults and obtained control of their land, they were encouraged to take out "subprime" mortgages that they could not afford. The improved lands then fell into the hands of local non-Indian business people at bargain prices. One potential Indian farmer named William Bundy fell victim to such tactics and lost all his property by age twenty-nine.[17]

One Miami was, for a time, successful. William Peconga became head of the Meshingomesia group after his grandfather's death. Peconga had an elementary education, attended a Baptist seminary at Ladoga, Indiana, and was a Mason. He skillfully managed the 1,500 acres of land his family received in allotments. When anthropologist Albert Gatschet visited him in the early 1890s, Peconga boasted of his good soil in which he grew corn, wheat, potatoes, peas, beans, tobacco, barley, and rye. Unfortunately, farm prices had sunk during the 1880s as new farming areas opened overseas. By 1892 Peconga, despite his best efforts, was deeply in debt. In 1898 he lost the last of his land and became a tenant farmer.[18] In 1903, thirty years after allotment, three Miami owned a total of only fifty-eight acres, 1 percent of the original reservation. The failure of Miami allotment was a harbinger of the failure of allotment nationwide after 1887, when millions of acres of Indian reservation land were suddenly converted to individual ownership.

The Miami on treaty grants near Peru, Indiana, fared better in the 1880s and 1890s. They were more acculturated to American ways and had managed their land for some time. In 1880 they owned nearly two thousand acres in many tracts. Peru sat at the intersection of three major railroads and was beginning rapid economic growth. Peru-area Miami could easily get casual jobs. In 1886 a wealthy livery stable owner named Benjamin Wallace bought a bankrupt circus and purchased land in the center of the Godfroy reserve as a winter quarters for a variety of animals. Miami men were soon hired to work on the circus farms and to tend animals. In 1891 Wallace purchased Gabriel Godfroy's 220-acre farm for a massive new circus winter quarters. From this prime location, Wallace's circuses departed on trains every spring and returned in the fall.[19]

In the midst of these changes, Gabriel Godfroy became the leader of the Peru-area Miami. Godfroy was prosperous and for many years had allowed landless Miami to live in small cottages on his property. Facing the burden of assisting poor tribespeople who were losing their annuity income in 1881, he challenged state taxation of treaty grants. He also sought repayment of $3,600 in taxes wrongfully collected on his treaty grants. In 1886 the federal district court of northern Indiana ruled that non-taxation was a right inherent in "their tribal relation."[20] In 1891 the Indiana Supreme Court affirmed non-taxation of treaty grants, and the state legislature prohibited taxation of such land so long as the Miami were not citizens.[21]

Further legal success came to the Miami concerning annuities paid to non-tribal members in the 1850s and 1860s. In 1895 the U.S. Court of Claims awarded the tribe $48,528 as reimbursement for the diverted annuities. Special Agent Marcus D. Shelby, who would later complete the roll for the Potawatomi of Michigan and Indiana, carefully made a new Miami roll in 1895. Each of the 440 Miami enrolled received $96 as his or her share.[22] Since the 1860s some Miami, nearly all descendants of Chief Richardville, had been moving west to Kansas and then to Indian Territory. In 1895 the Miami population in Indiana was 373, while 67 Indiana Miami now resided in the area of Miami, Indian Territory (now Oklahoma), among the western Miami who were removed in 1846. Shelby listed these tribal members separately. The western Miami tribe (removed in 1846) was only slightly larger than the Indiana immigrants, with 75 members.[23]

By the 1890s Indiana Miami children were attending federal Indian boarding schools at Carlisle, Pennsylvania, and Lawrence, Kansas. Such schools came in vogue after the Civil War as a way to assimilate Indian children to American ways. The Carlisle Indian Industrial School opened in 1879. Created by Richard Henry Pratt, a Civil War officer who had also led cavalry units on the Great Plains, Carlisle was intended to totally strip Indian children of their identity and to give them an American identity. Children were taken far from their homes and when school was not in session were put in the homes of nearby white farm families for further experiences in everyday American life. The Indian boarding schools have been roundly criticized for their harsh treatment of Indian children as young as five years old. At the same time, the schools taught skills that those Indians who survived the hazing could later use for the good of their tribes.

The Indiana Miami students who went to Carlisle and to Haskell Institute in Kansas were older, usually in their teens when they attended. They were more acculturated than students from western states and went by choice, as there was no Indian agent to force their attendance. Many of the Miami were children of tribal leaders who felt they could benefit from federal Indian education at a time when there were no local rural high schools and in a place where they would not face the prejudice common among whites. At the schools, the Miami met students from many other tribes and gained an understanding of national Indian issues.[24]

By coincidence, an Indian boarding school was located within five miles of the Meshingomesia reservation. White's Manual Labor Institute, a Quaker school chartered for "poor children, white, colored and Indian," was opened in 1870. Although there were plenty of poor Miami children in the vicinity, only one attended for a short time. The purpose of Indian education was to break the child's connection with home, and to do this, it was necessary to send the child far away. Therefore, children coming to White's were mostly Sioux children from reservations in Dakota Territory, while Miami children were sent to Kansas and Pennsylvania.

One eight-year-old girl came with great enthusiasm to White's Institute. Zitkala-Ša, later known as Gertrude Bonnin, arrived in 1884 at the age of eight. At first she was excited to come east to "the land of apples." However, she soon came to hate the "iron routine" of the school. Despite many difficulties, including seeing a classmate die, Zitkala-Ša graduated and went on to Earlham College in Richmond, Indiana. Illness forced her to quit Earlham, but not before she competed at the Indiana Oratorical Contest in Indianapolis and won second place in 1896. Although she went on to the New England Conservatory of Music and became an Indian activist, she was never fully at home in either American Indian or American culture. An ethnic identity as an Indian was not yet possible in the late nineteenth century. In 1902 she wrote an article for the *Atlantic Monthly* titled "Why I am a Pagan," shocking Americans who expected Indians to easily give up their religion.[25]

In 1896 Miami leaders decided to pursue the return of taxation wrongly imposed by the state of Indiana. If tribal leaders could succeed in obtaining the return of annuities that were wrongfully diverted, surely their solid legal position in regard to non-taxation of their lands would succeed also. The Miami met and appointed Camillus Bundy as spokesperson to take charge of the claim. At Bundy's request, Commissioner of Indian Affairs Daniel Browning reported that "the owners of this [treaty] land constitute a part of the Miami nation, and have kept up their tribal relations. . . . They are not citizens of the United States, and, indeed, could not rid themselves of their allegiance to their nation and become citizens without the consent of the United States." Browning concluded in his lengthy review of Miami legal status that the federal government should prosecute the case. The final step was a legal opinion from the head attorney of the Interior Department supporting the commissioner.[26]

Assistant Attorney General Willis Van Devanter rendered his decision on the Miami request for federal legal assistance on November 23, 1897. He ruled that the Indiana Miami had not been recognized since the Miami trust fund was distributed in 1881. Similar to the Catholic Potawatomi decision of 1866, Van Devanter ruled that this final payment also ended tribal relations for the Miami. According to Van Devanter, the Miami in the Peru area who had treaty grants were the same as allotted Indians. They had control of their land and were U.S. citizens, not tribal Indians. Therefore the federal government could not assist them in their claim against the state of Indiana.[27]

Zitkala-Ša (Gertrude Bonnin), a Sioux Indian from South Dakota, attended White's Institute near Wabash, Indiana, around 1890. She Attended Earlham College in Richmond, Indiana, for two years and won second place in the Indiana Oratorial Contest in 1896. In later life, she was a prominent Indian activist.

The Van Devanter decision had an immediate and devastating impact
on the Miami. Two generations of hard work by tribal leaders were suddenly
undone and every legal protection for the tribe ended. The decision effectively terminated the tribe and rendered the 1854 treaty meaningless. Within
months, Miami County commissioners appealed earlier cases exempting
treaty land from local taxation. The 1891 Indian law protecting treaty land
from taxes was overruled by the state supreme court. The Miami could "not be
both an Indian properly so-called and citizens."[28]

Within two months of Van Devanter's decision, word of the changed
status of the Miami spread to federal Indian schools. In January 1898 Judson
Peconga wrote from Haskell Institute to the Bureau of Indian Affairs, saying
that there was talk that "we the Miami Indians of Indiana have no right to
come here to school."[29] The students currently enrolled at Haskell and Carlisle
were allowed to stay, but when two Miami wanted to enter Haskell in 1901,
Commissioner of Indian Affairs Willis Jones replied that the government had
cut its connection with the tribe and was not going to "take a backward step
relative to these people." Jones then admitted that federal Indian schools had
failed in their goal to assimilate Indian children. He added, "To send them to
an Indian school would be simply to perpetuate their Indian characteristics,
and unquestionably would not be of advantage to the children."[30]

The 1890s were the low point for Indians across the United States. Allotment had become national policy with the passage of the General Allotment
Act in 1887. Like Indian removal in the 1830s, allotment was portrayed as a
liberal policy, a means of freeing Indians from communal ownership of land
and moving them into the mainstream of modern American life with private
ownership, away from tribalism and toward individualism. The reality was far
different. Between 1881 and 1900 Indian tribes nationally lost half of their
land, seventy-eight million acres. The Miami in Indiana faced allotment earlier
and consequently lost more of their land, 77 percent from 1880 to 1900 in the
area of core settlement between Peru, Wabash, and Marion.[31]

The Potawatomi of Michigan and Indiana kept their tribal federal recognition in 1900. They had, as citizens of Michigan, paid taxes on their private
landholdings since the 1840s. There was no basis for challenging state taxation
and in turn receiving a legal decision which destroyed their tribe. The Potawatomi were atypical in retaining their rights to government, or so it seemed for
a time.

7

Preserving Indian Ethnicity and Tribal Identity, 1900–1945

Come, see and hear the Indians tell their history in their own way.

Indiana Miami Pageant flyer, September 21, 1930

It was at the beginning of the twentieth century that ethnicity first became possible in any ordinary sense for American Indians. Indians, of course, would nearly always choose tribalism, with its protection of tribal land, values, and beliefs. American policy, however, supported the destruction of every element of tribalism in favor of assimilation. Indians who lost their tribal governments numbered in the tens of thousands in the early twentieth century. Without federal protection of their rights, they fell back to a second choice, that of asserting ethnicity. In most cases, Indians were asserting specific tribal ethnicity. Some Indians, however, looked to broader meanings of "Indianness." Often Indians shaping a new pan-Indian or general-ized Indian ethnicity lived in urban areas, had some or a great deal of educa-tion, and praised traditional values such as Indian closeness to nature while envisioning the Indian future in terms of professions, business, and modern farming. Their movement was based on appreciation of nature and coincided with the rise of conservation movements, the outdoors, and working with nature-oriented organizations like the Boy Scouts, Girl Scouts, and Camp Fire Girls.[1]

The Indiana Miami, like the Potawatomi of Michigan and Indiana, viewed themselves strictly in tribal, not ethnic terms. The ending of Miami tribal rights in Indiana in 1897 created a crisis as severe as Indian removal had fifty years earlier. Without legal protection as a tribe, the Indiana Miami were sud-denly and unexpectedly thrown on their own as an Indian group with very few resources. The Miami had a rich ethnic tradition, cultural and political, and were not about to quietly forget their Miami identity and disappear into the general population. They still had their 1854 treaty, which they saw as a "solemn obligation" of the U.S. government. The question became how to maintain Miami heritage and at the same time work to regain treaty rights.

Miami leaders began by creating their first formal organization, "The Tribe of Miami Indians of Indiana." They secured Chicago attorneys to press a claim to interest on the annuities taken from 1851 to 1867. The U.S. Department of the Interior supported the Miami claim, and government clerks calculated the interest owed the tribe to be $80,715. Legislation to fund the claim failed to pass in the U.S. House of Representatives, but the Miami were not deterred. They knew they were on the right track.[2]

Camillus Bundy, son of Peter Bondy (the spelling of their surname varies), was both a political and cultural leader of the Indiana Miami whose importance grew over the years after his father's death in 1895. Commonly known as "Kim," Bundy sensed the need to bring the Miami community more closely together. In 1903 he invited all tribal members to a reunion. Patterned somewhat after American family reunions, it was Indian in content. The location was moved from year to year to accommodate different tribal groups. The morning began with a tribal council meeting. At noon there was a community meal, then in the afternoon a general business meeting, followed by footraces and other games. People often wore tribal regalia, older people spoke the Miami language, and there was Indian dancing.[3]

By the early twentieth century, Miami children were attending local elementary schools. At the same time, Miami elders informally educated children in Miami folklore and beliefs. Public schooling must have seemed abstract and thin in comparison to the powerful lessons in Miami history, folklore, beliefs, and practical activities. Gabriel Godfroy and others told stories of the creation of the Miami, of giants and little people, and of the transformation of people and animals. Godfroy did not mind sharing with white audiences at times. One of his stories was published in the first issue of the *Indiana Magazine of History*.[4] The older Miami also taught history as they had experienced it. Some Miami leaders had met with U.S. presidents, whom they called *matatsopia*, "ten heads," perhaps referring to the executive departments presidents directed. Children became aware that history as the Miami lived it contrasted with history as it was taught in public school. One of Godfroy's lessons was that the

Miami "made peace with the whites in Washington's time and we never violated it. . . . The red men made their treaties and kept them, but the white men did not."[5] On occasion, heirlooms such as silver peace medals, original treaty documents, and old moccasins, leggings, and wampum belts were displayed and talked about as special tokens of Miami history.[6]

Albert Gatschet, a linguist with the Smithsonian, had visited the Miami in Indiana in the 1890s and began a study of the language, but died before he could finish the project. In 1905 Jacob Piatt Dunn, a journalist and gifted student of American Indian life, came from Indianapolis to the Miami community to continue Gatschet's language work. Dunn quickly realized that Miami was a dying language and began interviewing Godfroy and other Miami speakers, making word lists and notes on grammar. He also gathered stories, descriptions of games, and food ways of the Miami that had not been collected before. Dunn's work was exceptional, and Godfroy was acknowledged as the most fluent speaker of the Miami language.[7]

Godfroy's death in 1910 signaled the end of an era. As World War I approached, the rural Miami community began to break up as all but small fragments of Indian land were lost to sale and foreclosure. At the same time, new work opportunities opened up for the Miami in nearby Peru. A significant number of men worked for railroads on work crews and a few as locomotive firemen. In 1921 the Peru-area circuses, which included Hagenbeck-Wallace, John Robinson, Howe's Great London, and Sells-Floto, were reorganized as the American Circus Corporation, with much new equipment, as well as new barns on the former Gabriel Godfroy farm. Possibly the largest collection of wild animals in the world was gathered at the winter quarters. During the 1920s Miami men and women found work on circus farms, handling and feeding animals, and as costume seamstresses, concessionaires, and even performers.[8] Some Miami went "on the road" with circuses traveling in huge circus trains to all parts of the United States. One young Miami named Gabriel Tucker was killed while loading elephants in Sarasota, Florida, in 1923.[9] The circus world expanded the experience of Miami people, bringing them into contact with the world at large.

While Indians were romanticized in the early twentieth century, appearing on the nickel, gold coins, and a beautiful five-dollar bill, the reality was different. Geronimo, a prisoner of war, was put on display at the St. Louis World's Fair in 1904, his heart secretly aching for his Apache homeland in the

Victoria "Dooley" Brady, daughter of Camillus Bundy, was an Indiana Miami activist who tirelessly lobbied for Miami treaty rights during the 1920s.

COURTESY OF THE MIAMI NATION OF INDIANS OF INDIANA

mountains of Arizona. The Plains Indian wars and General George A. Custer's defeat were fresh in American minds. A few Indian celebrities were known, and various Wild West shows remained popular, but life for the vast majority of Indian people was harsh. As early movies began to stereotype all Indians as Plains warriors, many Indians lived quiet lives, keeping their heritage alive among themselves.

Indians across the United States began to disappear from the federal census as prejudice and economic conditions worsened in the twentieth century. In 1900 and again in 1910, the U.S. census included Indian schedules. The 1900 federal census recorded the low point of Indian population in American history—237,196. The census data were similar for Indiana. The 1900 Indian schedule listed 129 Miami in Miami County; 128 were listed in 1910. Although the Indian schedules of 1910 listed 128 Miami in Butler Township, Miami County, the U.S. census for 1910 gave a total of only 90 Miami Indians in the whole state, and the entire Indian population listed for Indiana in 1910 was 279. Besides the 90 Miami, there were 2 Delaware, 2 Wea, 1 Penobscot, and 184 Indians who did not report a tribe.[10] In the 1920 federal census for Indiana, only 125 people were identified as Indian for the whole state. At a time of rising intolerance in American society after World War I, it was safer to keep one's ethnic identity private. In 1924 all American Indians were made U.S. citizens. This seemingly progressive act was offset by continuing federal efforts to extinguish tribal ceremonies, allot reservation land, and eliminate tribal governments. Indians were welcomed as citizens, but, in turn, Indian ethnicity was meant to disappear.[11]

By the 1920s the Miami needed a new direction. Camillus Bundy, then in his seventies, was in danger of losing the last bit of his treaty land. In 1923 he called a general meeting of all Miami at his rural home to discuss the Miami grievances that had been building since the 1890s. These included taxation of land, interest on the annuities, and full treaty rights. Bundy was well situated to lead the tribe. His mother Ozahshinquah (Oonsaašinkwa) was a legendary figure in the tribe who had married five times, and children by each of her marriages had in turn married into five of the six Miami groups. Thus Bundy had intricate kinship ties through his siblings to nearly all Miami. Bundy had learned tribal leadership through his father Peter Bondy, who sat on the Miami tribal council from the 1850s until his death in 1895. Born in 1854, Bundy was at an age that lent him power as an elder. He was quietly known among the Miami to have the ability to communicate with ancestral leaders long dead and perhaps with animal spirits.[12]

When the last of Bundy's land was taken in 1924, he defended the graveyard of his ancestors as sacred land. His resistance seemed foolish to local whites, but his principled stand raised his status enormously among the many landless and powerless Miami. In order to continue the struggle for Miami rights, Bundy sold treasured heirlooms to museum collectors to pay for his personal lobbying in Washington, DC.[13] From 1925 to 1929 he and his daughter, Victoria "Dooley" Brady, traveled each year to the Bureau of Indian Affairs. Commissioner of Indian Affairs Charles Burke personally informed them repeatedly that the Miami had no rights as Indians. Burke went on to demean them personally, and shortly after Bundy petitioned President Calvin Coolidge for assistance in 1927, Burke assailed Bundy and Brady in a letter, telling them, "You have less of Indian than white blood, your lifetime has been spent in a white community, you have control of your own property, and for many years have been citizens of the United States."[14] In 1929, on her last visit to Washington, Brady staged a one-person occupation of the Bureau of Indian Affairs. She was evicted from the building when she attempted to search for documents personally. A memorandum circulated throughout the Bureau of Indian Affairs stated, "She no doubt knows that she cannot succeed in establishing any claim for the Indians, but she likes to stay in Washington—it is so much more pleasant than to stay at home and attend to her household affairs."[15]

In the summer of 1924 the Miami were invited to Greenville, Ohio, to present a pageant of Miami life at the site of the famous Greenville treaty signed by Little Turtle with General Anthony Wayne in 1795. The Miami created a village at the site, and the performance was so successful that the Miami began similar performances in northern Indiana with the intention of showing white audiences aspects of Miami culture while raising funds to pursue legal issues. The performance was named the Maconaquah Pageant in honor of the famous white captive Frances Slocum, and the Miami invited the general public to "come, see and hear the Indians tell their history in their own way." A flier advertising a 1930 pageant performance spoke of the "Mighty Miamis" who would sing Indian songs and stated that "old Indian life in general will be exemplified, including the Gay Indian costumes." The pageant was a cultural bridge to the non-Indian population that allowed the Miami the freedom to be themselves in a beneficial way. Miami men, women, and children participated until the pageant ended in the late 1930s.[16]

When Dooley Brady died in 1930, the *Indianapolis Star* and other prominent newspapers around the state asserted that the fight for Miami claims was over. They could not have been more wrong. Camillus Bundy and Dooley Brady, brave, courageous, and confrontational in the face of federal obstruction and defamation, had inspired a new wave of tribal activism and organization.[17] Wracked with arthritis, Kim Bundy retired from the leadership of Miami political and cultural activities after the death of his daughter. A new generation of leaders arose to take charge of Miami affairs. True to tribal ways, the leaders had learned at the feet of the previous generation and had firm kinship ties and the respect of the Miami people. Chief Elijah Marks was a great-nephew of Meshingomesia and bore the Miami name Mecatamungwah (Black Loon), the name of a respected Miami chief who died in the 1840s. Secretary-treasurer David Bondy, Camillus Bundy's son, had attended Carlisle Indian School. Regular council minutes were kept beginning in 1929. Meetings were held frequently in Marion and a business meeting at the annual Miami reunion. The new activists were in their forties and fifties and were keenly aware of tribal-federal relations back to the 1850s.[18]

Many Miami had lived in poverty since the 1880s, but the Great Depression brought deeper poverty and at times a sense of desperation.

The Maconaquah Pageant Players, pictured here ca. 1933, told Miami stories and recreated events in early Miami history to counter white stereotypes of the tribe.

Congressman Glenn Griswold wrote the Bureau of Indian Affairs in 1932 asking for relief of the Miami, "as there are many that are entirely destitute and in great need."[19] In the meantime, Elijah Shapp, a tribal council member, wrote to Senator Lynn Frazier, chair of the Committee on Indian Affairs, and every other possible federal official with some responsibility for Indian affairs concerning Miami hardships. In one of his many assertive but always proper letters he wrote, "I am going to keep on until we get justice." In September 1933 Shapp concluded a letter to Secretary of the Interior Harold Ickes with this chilling comment: "My people are starving."[20] Shapp and other Miami writing in the same vein were coolly informed that the Miami had no rights as Indians.

American Indian policy based on allotting reservations and ending Indian treaty rights had reached a crisis point by the time the administration of Franklin D. Roosevelt entered office in 1933. Making Indians citizens in 1924 had done nothing to alleviate the severe poverty, ill health, and lack of cultural or religious freedom for American Indians. Reservation Indians remained under the tight control of Indian agents and often could not leave the reservation without their permission. A national survey of all aspects of American Indian life published in 1928 revealed shocking conditions in Indian boarding schools, extremely high mortality among the Indian population, and a humiliating sense of powerlessness among Indian people generally. The Meriam Report, as it came to be known, pointed to the allotment of reservations as a key to the problem of Indian communities.[21] The Indiana Miami, whose land was allotted years before general allotment began in 1887, were poster children for the failure of a policy intended to make farmers of Indians at a time when many American farmers themselves could no longer sustain small family farms.[22]

The Meriam Report became the basis for what is known as the "Indian New Deal." In 1934 Congress passed the Indian Reorganization Act, or IRA, which redirected federal Indian policy. It remains the basis of American Indian policy today. Allotment was ended, most Indian boarding schools were closed, economic development funds were provided to tribes, and new local schools, clinics, and hospitals were built on reservations. Tribal governments were encouraged to modernize their organization and to create business committees to protect and develop tribal economic resources. The IRA left final decisions in the hands of the Bureau of Indian Affairs, but it encouraged local community control. In general, economic and social conditions on most reservations were far better when the Indian New Deal ended than they had ever been.[23]

Unfortunately for the Indiana Miami, Indian programs were restricted to federally recognized tribes. As living conditions among the Miami continued to deteriorate in the 1930s, regaining federal recognition took top priority. In 1936 the tribe found a tireless and effective lobbyist in the unlikely person of Nettie Blanche White. White was a minister in a spiritualist church in Wabash attended by a few Miami people. She was sympathetic to their plight and was authorized by the tribal council to act as "attorney in fact" to prod Washington for help. She was well organized and filed every document with the Department of the Interior. When she lobbied in Washington, DC, she took H. H. Evans, a capable Indiana attorney, along.[24]

White met with D'Arcy McNickle of the Tribal Organization Branch of the Bureau of Indian Affairs in 1937. McNickle apparently gave White solid advice on tribal organization, for when she returned to Indiana, the tribal council adopted a charter and bylaws very similar to those used by federally recognized tribes to modernize their governments. The Indiana secretary of state approved the tribal organization on September 30, 1937, under the name the Miami Nation of Indians of the State of Indiana.[25] The Miami Nation immediately introduced new claims legislation early in 1938. For the first time since 1910, the Department of the Interior reported favorably on Miami claims, with the suggestion to broaden the bill to include the Western Miamis. Congress did not pass the bill, which was reintroduced and failed to pass every year from 1938 to 1942, shot down by a small group of congressmen who routinely stopped similar claims legislation by other tribes year in and year out. With the failure to get claims heard and the federal court denial of treaty rights, the tribe found itself back where it had begun in 1897 when federal recognition was terminated.[26]

Mildred Bundy, a Miami graduate of Marion High School, wrote President Roosevelt in 1933 and put her finger on the problem from a Miami Indian perspective: "Have you ever heard of the Miami Indians? No doubt there are many there in Washington who have not. For years we have been forgotten, thrown aside as something not worth noticing. . . . I have seen many of my people go to their graves still professing that our government would do right by us. They never gave up hope. They were buried in poverty as they lived. . . . Isn't it about time we were recognized?"[27] Despite a reversal of old policies and much new help for Indian tribes, the Miami people remained mired for the most part in poverty and without much hope of improvement. Federal indifference left a legacy of anger among many Miami by the end of the 1930s. The officials of the Miami Nation, however, maintained a dignified stance toward the Washington bureaucracy. Shortly after Pearl Harbor, the Miami Nation passed a council resolution supporting the American war effort and ceased claims lobbying until the war was over.[28]

During this period from 1900 to 1945, the experience of the Potawatomi of Michigan and Indiana was far less dire than that of the Indiana Miami. The Potawatomi did not have a reservation for Congress to allot in the 1870s and therefore avoided congressional legislation that could have destroyed their federal recognition, as was the case with the Miami. In 1899 Simon Pokagon died. The grandson of Leopold Pokagon and son of Peter Pokagon, prominent earlier tribal leaders, Simon Pokagon had become a popular interpreter of Catholic Potawatomi culture and stories before the American public after losing a role in tribal government in the early 1880s. After his death, the tribe began to use the name Pokagon Potawatomi.

In the first three decades of the twentieth century, the Pokagon Potawatomi community continued much as it had earlier. The Indians were essentially rural, occupying small farms and other tracts of land in Cass, Van Buren, and Berrian counties in Michigan just over the state line from South Bend. Land loss was not an issue. The Potawatomi paid local taxes and made enough money from market gardening and other work to maintain their economic position without extreme hardship. There was work with tulip bulb growers, orchards, and vineyards, and some men entered military service during World War I. Others worked in war industries.[29]

As with the Miami, subsistence activities such as maple sugaring, gathering nuts and berries, hunting, and fishing remained important. During the 1920s the Potawatomi, like the Miami, hunted without state licenses, which was accepted by state game wardens. Among the Miami, tribal crafts had largely died out in the early twentieth century, but the Potawatomi made large quantities of baskets of all sizes. These were sold from homes or at local markets. Until the middle of the 1930s the Potawatomi brought loads of baskets to the University of Notre Dame in South Bend at Easter, Thanksgiving, and Christmas. For years the Pokagons supplied the university with all laundry baskets, wastebaskets, and any others that it needed. In turn, the university fed the Indians and provided each family with various food items. Many of the Potawatomi visiting Notre Dame honored their connection to the university by dressing in Indian regalia.[30]

For the most part, Potawatomi children attended Catholic schools and, to some extent, public schools. Few went to high school and only a few to Haskell Institute in Kansas. In the 1920s some parents sought and received permission for their children to attend the Indian boarding school at Mt. Pleasant, Michigan, approximately 125 miles from the tribal community. Graduates interviewed in the 1970s generally agreed that they received an excellent basic education. At the same time, they were exposed to the usual regimented daily life of such schools. The future benefit was getting to know Indians of other tribes and developing a broader identity as Native Americans and as Potawatomi.[31]

Up to the beginning of the Great Depression, the Potawatomi tribal council and business committee mainly concerned themselves with local matters of a community nature, such as organizing seasonal communal meals, weekend dancing, and social events. Occasionally harvest work on Indian farms was coordinated, and informal care of the elderly and help for the indigent offered. The Pokagons were long acculturated to independent self-reliance and making their own way with their own skills and knowledge. Like many Americans, they benefited from the prosperity of the 1920s. By the late 1920s most adults were employed as unskilled or semi-skilled workers in nearby factories in Dowagiac, St. Joseph, and Watervliet, while others worked in construction. Small-scale garden farming also remained important. The tribal population became more dispersed and, most likely, more Potawatomi moved to nearby towns.[32]

In 1929, with the coming of the Great Depression, economic conditions quickly became perilous. Although the Pokagons were federally recognized, they had no tribal land and had received none of the services of health clinics or tribal resource management of reservation tribes. At first they turned to limited state and local welfare resources. When the Roosevelt administration passed the IRA, many new resources became available to federally recognized Indian tribes, but funding and assistance went to tribes with reservation land.[33]

The Pokagon business committee was unaware of the bias in federal aid to tribes, and in 1934 quickly began the attempt to take part in the Indian New Deal. They soon learned that their chances were very slim. Like the Miami, but without the disability of being told that the federal government had no obligation to them, they bombarded the Secretary of the Interior, the Commissioner of Indian Affairs, and other federal officials. The Pokagons were informed that they would have to satisfy a "half-blood" quantum, that is, be a direct descendant of at least one full-blooded Native American or in some other way have half native ancestry.[34] This was an old racist concept of the Bureau of Indian

Affairs that was alien to their way of seeing themselves. The tribal leadership continued to try to get help, using different strategies. In the later 1930s federal surveys of Indian communities in Michigan were made that today offer a treasure trove of information. The results showed much poverty and poor economic and social conditions, but the Bureau of Indian Affairs did not have the funding to reach out to landless tribes, nor was there a legal mechanism to reach these tribes.

After years of back-and-forth correspondence, the Bureau of Indian Affairs concluded that the Potawatomi of Michigan and Indiana could not come under the IRA. The decision was galling because some landless Potawatomi in the Great Lakes area did get IRA recognition and aid, while the Pokagons, who had a treaty right to remain in Michigan, did not. As with the Indiana Miami, the Pokagon effort to get federal help during the Indian New Deal came to nothing, despite valiant efforts from 1934 to 1942. They took the defeat of their hard effort in stride, determined to return to the issue of full tribal recognition another day.[35]

8

The Rise of Modern Tribalism and American Indian Ethnicity, 1945–to the Present

I have, since my early years, listened to and talked with the older people, all now dead. We talked of those they knew and what they heard. And in that tradition passed along from the old to the young, we learned about those events and things that effected [sic] the whole Miami tribe.

Ira Sylvester Godfroy, in deposition for Indian Claims Commission, June 26, 1954, Peru, Indiana, Docket no. 124, the Miami Indian Tribe and Miami Tribe of Indiana v. the United States of America[1]

World War II was a great watershed in Indian affairs. More than twenty-five thousand American Indians from federally recognized tribes served in the military as well as many more thousands from non-federally recognized tribes. Thousands of Indian men and women moved to urban areas to work in war industries. American Indian people were exposed to the world at large, serving in integrated military units alongside white Americans. Though often called "chief," Indians in combat units gained the respect of their fellow servicemen through their courage and abilities, which were sometimes, as in the case of various tribal code talkers, quite specialized.

After World War II the pendulum of Indian policy began to shift away from the New Deal emphasis on reservation communities and tribal sovereignty. Impressed with the service of Indians in the war and concerned with their civil rights, both liberals and conservatives joined forces to create new federal policies to assimilate Indians into the mainstream of American society. The foundation of the new policy was to pay Indians for all past injustices, to remove Indians from reservations to cities, and to end all federal responsibilities to Indian tribes. The "Indian problem" would then be solved and justice served.

In 1946 Congress began the process with the Indian Claims Commission Act. A three-person board was created to review all treaty grievances against the federal government. The U.S. Department of Justice represented the federal government, while various lawyers, land appraisers, historians, and anthropologists represented the Indians. The claims commissioners then determined the awards. The House of Representatives followed up the claims legislation in 1953 with Concurrent Resolution 108, which called for eliminating treaty obligations, ending federal oversight of Indian affairs, and eliminating existing reservations. This part of the new policy became known as "termination." Indian tribes were not consulted on the new policy and were brushed aside when they protested. Finally, in 1952 the Bureau of Indian Affairs set up a relocation program to move Indians from reservations to large cities, where it was felt they would have better opportunities for education, work, and learning American ways.[2]

The Miami and the Potawatomi were ready after years of presenting claims to make use of the new claims legislation. Both tribes obtained the services of Walter Maloney, a Washington, DC, attorney experienced in Indian law. The claims process inched forward. In the Midwest there were so many competing claims among the Shawnee, Miami, Potawatomi, Delaware, Kaskaskia, Wea, Kickapoo, Six Nations Iroquois, and other tribes that the Great Lakes-Ohio Valley Project (GLOV) was organized at Indiana University in Bloomington to assist claimants. The enormous quantity of research required by tribal claims brought together cultural anthropologists and community-focused historians, creating a new specialty called ethnohistory. Indiana University was the focal point of much of the Great Lakes Indian claims research and also began publication of a new journal called *Ethnohistory* in 1954. The archives of this research remain at the Glenn A. Black Laboratory of Archaeology at Indiana University today.[3]

Settling Indian claims was meant to close out tribalism. Instead tribes that engaged in claims became revitalized. The Indiana Miami gained their first settlements in 1966 and 1969 for treaties from 1809 and 1818 in which the tribe was paid a few cents an acre rather than the $1.25 per acre the land of southern and central Indiana was worth at the time. The award, once expenses were deducted, amounted to a total of about $2,500 to each of the 3,066 people enrolled in the tribe. However, when adjusted for inflation, the shares were less than some nineteenth-century settlements.[4]

While claims activities energized tribes, city life encouraged Indians to look beyond tribes to shared Indian values and an expanding sense of Indian ethnicity. From 1952 to 1965, the Bureau of Indian Affairs relocated tens of thousands of poorer and less acculturated Indians from reservations to cities. Chicago, Seattle, Los Angeles, Denver, Minneapolis-St. Paul, and other cities acquired Indian populations larger than those on many reservations. Mostly living in ghettos, the new city dwellers struggled with poverty and cultural disorientation. Adam Fortunate Eagle, whose family moved to San Francisco when he was a child, wrote that "Indians began to find each other, partially out of loneliness and confusion in their new urban surroundings and partially out of an urge to share a cultural identity. First came the picnics in Golden Gate Park that grew into drumming and singing sessions. These grew into a powwow circuit of social gatherings that, often unconsciously, made their own subtle political statement of cultural unity and affirmation."[5]

With the arrival of the Lyndon B. Johnson administration and its War on Poverty, the federal government began substantial financial aid to urban Indian communities. The Office of Economic Opportunity, Comprehensive Employment Training Act, Indian Education Act, Administration for Native

The 1969–71 Indian occupation of Alcatraz brought national attention to issues of Indian rights.

Americans, and many other programs targeted urban as well as reservation
Indian communities. Educational and cultural programs led many Native
Americans living in cities to a much greater awareness of history and of their
own ethnicity. It was this sense of ethnic awareness and empowered leadership that led to the first Indian studies programs at the University of Califor-
nia, Berkeley, and at other universities. Urban Indian activism and Red Power,
an activist movement by pan-Indian groups, brought about a new identity
beyond tribal identity and encouraged many people of Native American
heritage to assert an Indian ethnic identity.[6]

Urban Indians, who in the 1950s and 1960s formed hundreds of community groups, were caught up in a powerful sense of injustice fueled by federal
policies against tribes and also were inspired by the civil rights movement.
Activism grew during the 1960s with "fish ins" in the Northwest protesting
loss of fishing rights and demonstrations for restoring federal recognition to
terminated tribes. A new organization, the American Indian Movement (AIM),
joined tribal grievances with urban grievances. Founded in 1968 in Minneapolis-St. Paul, Minnesota, in the middle of a multi-tribal Indian community
of more than ten thousand people, AIM began by protesting police harassment. AIM quickly broadened its confrontational tactics against stereotyping
of Indians, broken treaties, and lack of Indian self-determination on reservations. Under the stimulus of the new activism, Indians raised in cities were
soon visiting reservations and gaining an awareness of "Indianness" from
tribal elders, while they confronted bureaucratic arrogance head-on, giving
hope to reservation Indians.[7]

Activism culminated in Indian occupation of the former federal prison at
Alcatraz Island in San Francisco Bay beginning in November 1969 and lasting nineteen months, until June 1971. Alcatraz marked the beginning of the
Red Power period of American Indian history. The occupation gained national
attention, and for the first time many Americans saw Indians on the nightly
news. Alcatraz had an electrifying impact on Indian participants. Wilma
Mankiller's family was relocated from Oklahoma to San Francisco in the late
1950s. Later chief of the Oklahoma Cherokee, she wrote:

> "I must always remember where the journey started. It was in San Fran-
> cisco—at Alcatraz, and at the American Indian Center, and in my own
> home where, starting about the time of the Alcatraz takeover, native people
> often came to sip coffee, make plans, and build indestructible dreams. The

*occupation of Alcatraz excited me like nothing ever had before. It helped
to center me and caused me to focus on my own rich and valuable
Cherokee heritage."*[8]

Ironically, the federal relocation program, meant to take Indians far from
tribal roots, often created the motivation for revitalizing those roots.

With activism and a new sense of pride among Native Americans, the
Indian population grew rapidly on U.S. census enumerations. Traditionally,
Native American ethnicity focused on tribalism, that is, enrollment in or
allegiance to a particular Indian nation. After World War II, however, a more
general sense of being Native American grew. Connection to a particular
tribe remained strong, but to outsiders and in the public arena, it was easier
to identify as Native American or Indian. Before 1960 census enumerators
decided what category people fit: white, black, or Indian, to name the major
three. From 1930 to 1950 the "official" Indian population of the United States
barely grew, by only a little over 14,000 (4 percent) to a total of 357,499.[9] In
1960, however, the census bureau allowed people to identify the racial group
they belonged to. With self-identification, the Indian population reported in
1960 suddenly jumped by 46 percent from 1950, to 523,591. The 1970 census
showed another large increase, 51 percent, to 792,730. The 1980 increase
was the largest, 72 percent, or 571,000, for a total of 1,363,033. In 1990 the
increase slowed to 38 percent, the Indian population rising to 1,878,285.[10]

Indiana far outdid the increase in national figures from 1930 to 1990. The
state Indian population grew from 285 in 1930 to 438 in 1950 (153 percent)
and in 1960 more than doubled to 948 (216 percent). From 1960 to 1970 the
population more than quadrupled to 3,887 (410 percent). In 1980 the state
Indian population nearly doubled again, to 7,682 (198 percent). The increase
slowed in 1990 to 165 percent, reaching 12,720.[11] Clearly and surprisingly,
Indiana had far outpaced the growth in Indian ethnicity nationally. For
whatever reason, the state was a magnet for Indians from other areas and
was a desirable environment for being Indian. Indiana was truly living up to its
name as "Land of the Indians." We will return to this theme later.

Several factors contributed to the national rise in American Indian population beginning in 1960. In earlier years, pressure to assimilate and prejudice
against Indians clearly led to a large under-enumeration. Undoubtedly, the
lessening of prejudice against Indians and the growth of Native American
pride led many people to identify as Indian who previously had kept their

identity private. Racial self-identification on the 1960 federal census was an invitation to assert Indian identity, and many people did so. For a large proportion of people of mixed race, Indian ethnicity became more important while prejudice against Indians as a race lessened, encouraging many people to assert their identity as American Indian.[12] After the Indian Health Service was placed within the U.S. Public Health Service in 1955, health care on reservations improved and Indian life expectancy increased. Natural increase may account for somewhat over half of the increase from 1960 to 1980. Better enumeration of Indians living on reservations also probably added to the increase.[13] It is impossible to quantify each of these changes. In the larger picture, American Indian ethnicity was part of a growing trend of ethnic identity among a multitude of subcultures in the United States. For example, while the growth of the American Indian population was high, the growth in numbers and rates of growth for Asian/Pacific Islanders and Hispanics were far higher.[14]

Indiana offered alternatives to confrontational Indian activism. There were no longer reservations. The fact that the state was not selected for relocation of Indians meant that Indians made a personal choice to move to the state. If

Now restored by the Miami Tribe of Indiana, this schoolhouse built by Chief Meshingomesia in 1860 is located on the former Miami reservation near Marion, Indiana. The school served Indian and white children near Marion until 1898.

PHOTO BY RICHARD FIELDS, COURTESY OF DNR, *OUTDOOR INDIANA*, MARCH/APRIL 2008 they liked the move—and many did—they could invite other family or tribal members to move to Indiana as well. The state was a magnet of choice because Indians did not have to fight state and local authorities to carve out political space and identity; their identity was accepted. Likewise, the Red Power movement and AIM militancy never caught on among the Miami, Potawatomi, and Shawnee Indians of Indiana. Jan Hammil, who represented American Indians Against Desecration, a branch of AIM, attempted to stir up militancy among the Indians of Indiana concerning university research into ancient Indian human remains. Her reasoning for targeting Indiana was that "[Indiana] is kind of right here in the center of things."[15] Her aggressive tactics, however, angered Indian spokespeople. Howard LaHurreau, a Potawatomi and roadman (minister) of the Native American Church, said, "Often times people go off half-cocked with a good idea and the good idea gets lost in the process."[16] LaHurreau and representatives of the Miami and Shawnee informed Hammil that their solution was for Indiana tribes and state and university officials to jointly determine the disposition of skeletal remains.[17] Hammil left Indiana soon after the tribal rebuff.[18]

In 1987 the protection of ancient Indian remains became critical when pothunters and professional grave looters destroyed burial sites in western Kentucky. The cooperative approach between Indians and state officials worked well. Ray White (then chairman of the Indiana Miami) joined Dennis Banks, one of the founders of AIM, to lobby the Kentucky and Indiana legislatures for strong protection of Indian burial sites. Both states passed legislation making destruction of prehistoric burial sites (pre-1850) a felony offense. Unfortunately, the legislation did not pass in time to prevent the destruction of Windsor Mound, a large prehistoric burial site east of Muncie in Randolph County, Indiana. It should be added that White and Banks encouraged protecting historic non-Indian sites as well by using the date 1850 as a cutoff point.[19] In 1990 Congress passed the Native American Graves Protection and Repatriation Act, adding federal protection to Indian grave sites and calling for return of human remains and sacred objects identified with federally recognized tribes to those tribes.[20]

On July 8, 1970, President Richard Nixon reversed the policy of termination and declared the beginning of self-determination for American Indian tribes. In a special message to Congress, he stated:

> *"It is long past time that the Indian policies of the Federal government began to recognize and build upon the capacities and insights of the Indian*

*people. Both as a matter of justice and as a matter of enlightened social
policy, we must begin to act on the basis of what the Indians themselves
have long been telling us. The time has come to break decisively with the
past and to create the conditions for a new era in which the Indian
future is determined by Indian acts and Indian decisions."*[21]

Nixon went on to press Congress to pass legislation that would allow
tribes to take over the control and operation of federally funded programs
from the Bureau of Indian Affairs and other federal agencies. The intention
was to hand over the operation of many day-to-day programs to tribes.
Turning federal policy away from termination of tribal rights and toward
self-determination was a decisive turning point in American Indian history.
Federal recognition suddenly took on new meaning with the empowerment
of tribes through federal protection of tribal rights and support from an array
of federal agencies.

Federal backing of tribal sovereignty and self-determination gave real
power to federally recognized tribes. Unlike all other ethnicities in the United
States, Indian people who are members of tribes recognized by the federal government are citizens of tribal governments with specific powers under federal
Indian law to protect and enhance their communities. Federal tribes have their
own Indian police and court systems, control adoptions of Indian children,
and manage tribal schools and businesses. In short, they are another level
of government alongside cities, counties, and states, with their own specific
governing powers. Under federal law, they are not subject to many state civil
laws. In 1991 President George H. W. Bush asserted that "[t]his government-
to-government relationship is the result of sovereign and independent tribal
governments being incorporated into the fabric of our Nation . . . and [has]
evolved into a vibrant partnership in which over 500 tribal governments
stand shoulder to shoulder with the other governmental units that form
our Republic."[22]

We now come full circle to the Indians of Indiana, tribal and ethnic. The
reader may recall that the Indiana Miami and the Pokagon Potawatomi both
lost their federal status, the Miami through a legal ruling in 1897 and the
Potawatomi through federal neglect at the beginning of the twentieth century.
Both tribes failed to regain federal recognition in the 1930s, but with the birth
of the policy of self-determination in 1970, the tide was turning in their favor.
In 1978 the Bureau of Indian Affairs set up a procedure by which unrecognized tribes could petition for federal recognition. To become recognized,

Two Potawatomi confer at a 1971 powwow on the University of Notre Dame campus.

claimants had to show that they had always been considered Indian, that they inhabited a specific area and were a community, and that they had maintained political influence over their members.[23]

The Miami notified the Branch of Acknowledgment and Recognition (BAR) of their intent to petition in 1979, and the Pokagon Potawatomi did the same in 1982. Both tribes set about sponsoring meetings to inform their members, applying for grants to support expert research, and assembling volunteers for assistance. Both tribes were top candidates from the beginning for federal recognition. The Miami filed their petition in 1984, and it was praised as a model for other groups to follow. The Potawatomi filed their petition a few years later. In the meantime, both tribes established their first offices and increased services to members. By 1990 the Miami had moved to a large office complex at the old Peru High School on Miami Street in Peru. There they held council meetings, sponsored meals for the elderly and tribal bingo, and operated a daycare center.[24] The Potawatomi established a similar office at Silver Creek, Michigan. Ray White of the Miami and Phil Alexis of the Pokagon Band directed an increasing number of tribal activities while the tribes continued to work with the Bureau of Indian Affairs on their petitions.[25]

As the late 1980s wore on, the BAR seemed to bog down in tribal petitions, while adding layers of questions to the petitioners. Finally, on July 12, 1990, the Miami were informed that the tribe did not meet two of the criteria: sufficient evidence of governance and evidence of a distinct Indian community.[26] Surprisingly, the Bureau of Indian Affairs declared that the 1897 Van Devanter decision was wrong. The Miami had not lost their federal recognition, as congressional legislation in 1873 and 1881 had not "severed Miami tribal relations, or even hinted that the Government was attempting to sever those relations."[27] For more than ninety years the Bureau of Indian Affairs had repeatedly told the Miami they were not recognized. Now it seemed they were told that the tribal community no longer effectively governed a distinct tribal community. The Miami found this mockery of the epic and heroic efforts of earlier leaders to regain treaty rights impossible to understand and emotionally devastating. In the larger community of scholars of Indian law, the denial of Miami recognition was particularly controversial in light of the tribe's extensive documentation and treaty relations with the United States.[28]

On June 9, 1992, the Bureau of Indian Affairs made a final determination against federal recognition of the Indiana Miami. The Miami then sued the

Department of the Interior and began a nine-year legal process in the federal court system. In a series of four rulings, the federal district court for northern Indiana at South Bend ruled for the government and against the Miami. The tribe then appealed the decision to the Seventh District Court in Chicago. In June 2001 the Seventh District ruled against the Miami. Judge Richard Posner wrote that the Miami tribal government "operates a number of programs concerned with welfare (such as day-care programs) and economic develop-ment, and it has sought and obtained grants to fund these programs. But such programs, charitable rather than administrative in character, are a far cry from 'governance.'" He acknowledged a tribal council, "but it performs no meaning-ful governance functions."[29] His words eerily echoed similar judicial decisions a century earlier when federal courts often declared tribal governments did not govern, therefore tribes had abandoned tribal relations—and treaty rights. The U.S. Supreme court refused to review the appeal in 2002.[30]

The Pokagon Potawatomi, frustrated with the federal recognition process, withdrew their petition in disgust in 1991. Congressmen Fred Upton of Michi-gan and Tim Roemer of Indiana introduced a recognition bill in Congress. The tribe then hired Washington lobbyist Karl Funke to work their bill through Congress along with the bills of two other Michigan tribes. Three years later, in September 1994, Congress recognized the Pokagon Band of Potawatomi of Michigan as a tribe. President Bill Clinton met Phil Alexis and tribal leaders at the White House for the signing of the legislation. With federal recognition, the Pokagon Potawatomi immediately begin to build a modern tribal com-munity with headquarters at Dowagiac. The new tribal service area included four Michigan counties and six Indiana counties: La Porte, St. Joseph, Elkhart, Starke, Marshall, and Kosciusko. In 1997 the tribe began buying land in south-western Michigan for reservation development.[31] With federal recognition of the Pokagon Potawatomi, Indiana had a tribal jurisdiction inside the state for the first time in many years.

Apart from tribalism, the growth of Indian ethnicity in Indiana, and nationally, remains dynamic. The old notion of a one-way road to total assimi-lation was no longer viable—if it ever had been. Indian people have continued to believe in their right to be Indians in America. The fact that the federal government attempted to destroy Indian values and ways of life for two hun-dred years has probably strengthened Indian ethnicity today. No other group in American society has faced warfare, ethnic cleansing, boarding schools, legal denial of the practice of its religion, large-scale removal of children from families to be raised as whites, and massive loss of land and resources from the federal government. Indian memories are long, encouraging vigilance against any attempts to go back to the bad days of a past that is still recent in many memories.

Conclusion

Rebecca Martin is an Acoma Pueblo woman, raised traditionally on the reservation in northern New Mexico where many of her family still live. Her mother is an honored Clan Mother, and other family members are Medicine Women and active in tribal government. At the same time, she has lived for many years in Indianapolis and owns a business on the north side of the city dedicated to Native American and Southwestern art, jewelry, and interior décor. She describes Indiana as "a laid back place" and Indianapolis as a city with many advantages for Indian people. Unlike cities such as Chicago and Minneapolis, which were destinies for Indians relocated by the federal government from reservations, she feels Indianapolis has been free from much of the prejudice of cities with larger Indian populations. In general, she feels Indiana has attracted many Indian people because Indiana is a relaxed place for Indian people with many job opportunities.[1]

The 2000 federal census for Indiana shows a strong rise in the Indian population for the state. The number of people in Indiana who selected "American Indian or Alaska Native" as their only race rose to 15,815 from 12,720 in 1990 (24 percent). In addition, 23,448 people selected "American Indian or Alaska Native and another race," for a total of 39,263. The increase for Indiana in 2000 for those declaring another race along with Indian was slightly more than three times as many people as reported "Indian and Alaska Native" alone in 1990. In contrast, the increases for Michigan were much lower. Michigan, unlike Indiana, has reservations and twelve federally recognized tribes. There, the increase for those reporting one race in 2000 rose only five percent over 1990. Those reporting more than one race doubled.[2] These numbers seem to confirm Martin's impression. While Michigan has many more Indians than Indiana, the Indian population in Indiana is increasing far more rapidly.

The Indian population of Indiana is a complex mixture today. In the 2000 census, some 25,000 people specified connections with more than 150 tribes. Around 13,000 people identified themselves as American Indian, but did not specify a particular tribe. Just over 1,000 Latin American Indians were included. Though greatly outnumbered by the Cherokee, 2,377 reported Miami as their tribe, and 597 reported Potawatomi.[3] The Miami remained a significant presence as the second-largest group of Indians as well as through their many activities as a tribe.

The very large number of tribes represented in Indiana suggests that the state is not only the crossroads of America, but the crossroads of Indian America as well. Interestingly, the state has been an Indian crossroads as far back as the seventeenth century. In some ways, not much has changed in more than three centuries. The expectation over much of that time has been that Indians would disappear, either through voluntary or involuntary moves to the West, through alcoholism and disease, or through assimilation. Such has not been the case. Indians of many tribal backgrounds and from tribally conservative to highly progressive have been a presence in Indiana to a greater or lesser degree for a very long time. They have "changed with the changes" and asserted their presence in modern, increasingly multicultural America. Significantly, throughout the comings and goings of Native people, the Miami have maintained a strong presence in Indiana.

Since the 1970s half of American Indians have lived in cities.[4] By 2000, if not earlier, the same was true for Indiana. Rural counties typically count few Indians, whereas Indianapolis (Marion County) now has the largest number, followed by Lake, Allen, and St. Joseph counties. The one exception is Miami County, with the largest population of Miami Indians in the state. Miami County is also the only county in Indiana to have more than 1.5 percent Indian population.[5]

Urbanism and American Indian ethnic identity are closely related. A general sense of Indian ethnicity grew out of the mix of Indians who moved to cities during World War II and who were joined in the 1950s by tens of thousands of other Indians relocated by the federal government. People from dozens of tribes rubbed shoulders at Indian centers, in churches, and in urban powwows. As people married between tribes, tribal identities became more complex. Though tribal identities remained important, it became easier to tell outsiders that one was simply "Indian."[6] At the same time, a profusion of Indian community associations along with federally funded health and job programs created a network of support for Indian ethnic identity apart from tribalism. The establishment of Indian commissions in many cities and states in the 1970s provided a central forum for presenting Indian needs and concerns that enhanced ethnic awareness and effectiveness. Indian commissions are invariably multi-tribal and take on some of the aspects of an urban tribal government; that is, the Indian commissions have an important role in defining what urban Indian ethnicity is and what its boundaries are. In short, they enhance among Indians and before the general public what defines "Indianness."[7]

Indiana has lagged behind other states in the institutions that support Indian ethnicity but is catching up. In 2003 the state legislature created the Indiana Native American Indian Affairs Commission, charged with studying and making recommendations to local, state, and federal governments concerning a wide of array of Indian issues. In 2009 Brian Buchanan, chief of the Miami Nation of Indiana, is chairman. The commission meets in Indianapolis, which is also the site of the Eiteljorg Museum of American Indian and Western Art. The Eiteljorg has created a permanent exhibit on the Indians of Indiana and also sponsors an Indian Fair every summer, as well as workshops by a variety of nationally known Indian artists.

The tribal headquarters of the Miami Nation is in Peru, Indiana, at the center of the tribal population along the upper Wabash River. The tribe, though not federally recognized, sponsors many activities, including an "All Nations Gathering" on tribal lands in Parke County. Tribal committees handle enrollment, college scholarships, business, and cultural activities. The tribe is responsible for several tribal cemeteries and has restored the schoolhouse built in the 1860s with the encouragement of then Chief Meshingomesia, located on the land of the Meshingomesia cemetery.[8] The language committee sponsors Winter Stories in January, open to tribal members only, as well as language camps. A new summer language camp for Miami youngsters aged ten to sixteen has been started at the Indiana Dunes National Lakeshore.[9] The focus on tribal members is important because the Miami, like many tribes, are recreating a sense of community and belonging that builds confidence and esteem among tribal members of all ages and ensures continuity of the tribe into the future. The Indiana Miami tribe continues to seek federal acknowledgment of the treaty of 1854. The tribe has never ceased defending treaty rights, seen as a solemn obligation of the federal government. The future of the Indiana Miami tribe is secure, but federal Indian law would greatly enhance the ability of the tribe to provide services to its members.

The Pokagon Band of Potawatomi, while headquartered in Dowagiac, Michigan, has, as mentioned earlier, a six-county service area for its members in northern Indiana. Recognized by the federal government in 1994, in 1997 the tribe acquired 4,700 acres of land in three tracts just north of the Indiana state line in Michigan for reservation development. With an economic base a tribe is better able to serve its membership with many different community services. Typically these include education, health, child welfare, jobs, tribal police and courts, and assistance for the elderly.[10] In August 2007 the

Pokagon Band opened the Four Winds Casino at New Buffalo, Michigan, a short distance from the Indiana state line near Interstate 94 and within easy reach of the cities of northwest Indiana and the Chicago region.[11] Some have called Indian casinos the modern version of the buffalo, a generator of cash flow that can aid every type of community project in today's world.

Indiana is blessed with a rich Indian ethnicity that in many ways is more evident and dynamic today than ever before. It is expressed through tribalism and a sense of Indian nationality as well as in ethnic identity as Indian. Today's Hoosier Indians of whatever background have by and large chosen to live in Indiana. Through their traditions and activities they enrich the lives of all of us. They look to the future as well as to the past, confident, as one man said, "that we will always be here."

Notes

INTRODUCTION

1. Elizabeth J. Glenn and Stewart Rafert, "Native Americans," in *Peopling Indiana: The Ethnic Experience*, ed. Robert M. Taylor Jr. and Connie A. McBirney, 392–419 (Indianapolis: Indiana Historical Society, 1996).

2. Stewart Rafert, *The Miami Indians of Indiana: A Persistent People, 1654–1994* (Indianapolis: Indiana Historical Society, 1996); Bert Anson, *The Miami Indians*, The Civilization of the American Indian Series, vol. 103 (Norman: University of Oklahoma Press, 1970); James A. Clifton, *The Prairie People: Continuity and Change in Potawatomi Indian Culture, 1665–1965* (Lawrence: Regents Press of Kansas, 1977); R. David Edmunds, *The Potawatomis: Keepers of the Fire* (Norman: University of Oklahoma Press, 1978).

3. Arrell M. Gibson, *The Kickapoos: Lords of the Middle Borders* (Norman: University of Oklahoma Press, 1963).

4. Clinton A. Weslager, *The Delaware Indians: A History* (New Brunswick, NJ: Rutgers University Press, 1972), chapter 14; Amy C. Schutt, *Peoples of the River Valleys: The Odyssey of the Delaware Indians* (Philadelphia: University of Pennsylvania Press, 2007).

5. Roger James Ferguson, "The White River Indiana Delaware: An Ethnohistoric Synthesis, 1795–1867" (PhD diss., Ball State University, 1972).

6. Bruce G. Trigger, ed., *Northeast*, vol. 15, *Handbook of North American Indians*, (Washington, DC: Smithsonian Institution, 1978).

7. Henry F. Dobyns and William R. Swagerty, *Their Number Become Thinned: Native American Population Dynamics in Eastern North America* (Knoxville: University of Tennessee Press in cooperation with the Newberry Library Center for the History of the American Indian, 1983). The view generally held by Europeans from the time of the earliest Spanish explorers was that the interior of the North American continent was sparsely settled in pre-historic times. However, current scholarship in archaeology and anthropology negates this view.

8. Charles E. Cleland, *Rites of Conquest: The History and Culture of Michigan's Native Americans* (Ann Arbor: University of Michigan Press, 1992); Robert E. Bieder, *Native American Communities in Wisconsin, 1600–1960: A Study of Tradition and Change* (Madison: University of Wisconsin Press, 1995).

CHAPTER 1:
The Original Ethnic Groups of Indiana, 9500 BC–1670 AD

1. Louis Hennepin, *A Description of Louisiana*, trans. John G. Shea (NY: John G. Shea, 1880), 140.

2. Pierre Margry, *Découvertes et établissements des Français dans l'ouest et dans le sud de l'Amérique Septentrionale (1614–1754)* (Paris: D. Jouaust, 1876), 1:116; Bruce G. Trigger, ed., *Northeast*, vol. 15, *Handbook of North American Indians* (Washington, DC: Smithsonian Institution, 1978), 588–89.

3. Reuben G. Thwaites and Joseph P. Donnelly, *The Jesuit Relations and Allied Documents: Travels and Explorations of the Jesuit Missionaries in New France, 1610–1791* (Cleveland, OH: Burrows, 1898), 59:145.

4. There are few recent syntheses of Indiana's prehistory. The most recent with that intention is James H. Kellar, *An Introduction to the Prehistory of Indiana* (Indianapolis: Indiana Historical Society, 1973). A collection of articles providing more recent interpretations of some periods of

central Indiana prehistory is Ronald Hicks, ed., *Native American Cultures in Indiana: Proceedings of the First Minnetrista Council for Great Lakes Native American Studies* (Muncie, IN: Minnetrista Cultural Center, 1992). A brief summary is contained in James R. Jones III and Amy L. Johnson, *Early Peoples of Indiana*, rev. ed. (Indianapolis: Indiana Department of Natural Resources, Division of Historic Preservation and Archaeology, 2008).

5. John T. Dorwin, *Fluted Points and Late-Pleistocene Geochronology in Indiana*, vol. 4, no. 3, Prehistory Research (Indianapolis: Indiana Historical Society, 1966). A fluted point is a spear point upon which the hafting element, near the base, has been modified by striking large flakes vertically from the base and bilaterally, on two sides of the base. This thins the base for attaching to a shaft or handle.

6. Donald R. Cochran, "Adena and Hopewell Cosmology: New Evidence from East Central Indiana," in *Native American Cultures in Indiana* (see note 4), 26–40. Archaeoastronomy concerns interpreting archaeological earthworks (or stone works) or their features in terms of their alignment with the movements of stars, sun, moon, and so forth (i.e., astrological phenomena).

7. A full description of this site is found in Glenn A. Black, *Angel Site: An Archaeological, Historical, and Ethnological Study* (Indianapolis: Indiana Historical Society, 1967).

8. An examination of this issue has been made by James Allison Brown and Patricia J. O'Brien, eds., *At the Edge of Prehistory: Huber Phase Archaeology in the Chicago Area* (Kampsville, IL: Center for American Archaeology for the Illinois Department of Transportation, 1990), 155–60. Brown elaborates his position in John A. Walthall and Thomas E. Emerson, eds., *Calumet & Fleur-de-lys: Archaeology of Indian and French Contact in the Midcontinent* (Washington, DC: Smithsonian Institution Press, 1992), 77–128.

9. Ives Goddard, ed., *Languages*, vol. 17, *Handbook of North American Indians* (Washington, DC: Smithsonian Institution, 1996), 583–87.

10. Trigger, ed., *Northeast* (see note 2). Cultural descriptions and historical summaries of all the tribes associated with Indiana are found throughout the book under their familiar tribal names.

11. An excellent treatment of the history of Indiana during the pre-statehood period is John D. Barnhart and Dorothy L. Riker, *Indiana to 1816: The Colonial Period*, vol. 1, The History of Indiana (Indianapolis: Indiana Historical Bureau and Indiana Historical Society, 1971). A collection of articles pertaining to the contest for continent from the perspective of the Indiana region is found in John B. Elliott, ed., *Contest for Empire, 1500–1775: Proceedings of an Indiana American Revolution Bicentennial Symposium, Thrall's Opera House, New Harmony, Indiana, May 16 and 17, 1975* (Indianapolis: Indiana Historical Society, 1975).

CHAPTER 2:
France, England, and The Fur Trade, 1670–1783

1. Emma Helen Blair, *The Indian Tribes of the Upper Mississippi Valley and Region of the Great Lakes: As Described by Nicolas Perrot, French Commandant in the Northwest; Bacqueville de la Potherie, French Royal Commissioner to Canada; Morrell Marston, American Army Officer; and Thomas Forsyth, United States Agent at Fort Armstrong* (Lincoln: University of Nebraska Press, 1911; repr., 1996), 330–32.

2. W. Vernon Kinietz, *The Indians of the Western Great Lakes, 1615–1760* (Ann Arbor: University of Michigan Press, 1965) provides an example of reconstruction of the Miami and Potawatomi cultures from early French sources.

3. For a detailed description of the fur trade in Indiana, see Bert Anson, "The Fur Traders in Northern Indiana, 1796–1850" (PhD diss., Indiana University, 1953); For a developmental

discussion see Elizabeth J. Glenn, "Miami and Delaware Trade Routes and Relationships in Northern Indiana," in *Native American Cultures in Indiana: Proceedings of the First Minnetrista Council for Great Lakes Native American Studies*, ed. Ronald Hicks, 58–70 (Muncie, IN: Minnetrista Cultural Center, 1992).

4. Dean L. Anderson, "Variability in Trade at Eighteenth-Century French Outposts," in *French Colonial Archaeology: The Illinois Country and the Western Great Lakes*, ed. John A. Walthall, 218–36 (Urbana: University of Illinois Press, 1991). Anderson compares the trade goods actually available at Ouiatenon with those from other French posts.

5. Joseph L. Peyser, ed. and trans., *Letters from New France: The Upper Country, 1686–1783* (Urbana: University of Illinois Press, 1992), 100–102.

6. Emma Helen Blair, ed., *The Indian Tribes of the Upper Mississippi Valley and Region of the Great Lakes* (Cleveland, OH: Arthur H. Clark, 1969), 322–34.

7. T. J. Brasser, "Huron," in *Northeast*, ed. Bruce G. Trigger, vol. 15, *Handbook of North American Indians*, 204–5 (Washington, DC: Smithsonian Institution, 1978).

8. Lucien Campeau, "Roman Catholic Missions in New France," in *History of Indian-White Relations*, ed. Wilcomb E. Washburn, vol. 4, *Handbook of North American Indians*, 464–71 (Washington, DC: Smithsonian Institution, 1988).

9. Helen Hornbeck Tanner and Miklos Pinther, *Atlas of Great Lakes Indian History*, vol. 174, The Civilization of the American Indian (Norman: Published for the Newberry Library by the University of Oklahoma Press, 1987), 169–71.

10. State Historical Society of Wisconsin, *Collections of the State Historical Society of Wisconsin* (Madison, WI: State Historical Society of Wisconsin, 1908), 181, 185, 322–26.

11. Elisabeth Tooker, "Wyandot," in *Northeast* (see note 7), 400.

12. Frances Krauskopf, ed. and trans., *Ouiatanon Documents* (Indianapolis: Indiana Historical Society, 1955), 206–7; Paul Woehrmann, *At the Headwaters of the Maumee: A History of the Forts at Fort Wayne* (Indianapolis: Indiana Historical Society, 1971), 5–11. An interesting local view is in Bert Joseph Griswold and Samuel R. Taylor, *The Pictorial History of Fort Wayne, Indiana: A Review of Two Centuries of Occupation of the Region about the Head of the Maumee River* (Chicago: Robert O. Law, 1917), 42–44.

13. Lucy Elliot Keeler, "Old Fort Sandoski of 1745 and the 'Sandusky Country,'" *Ohio Archaeological and Historical Quarterly* 17 (October 1908): 357–430.

14. The 1748 treaty is in Alden T. Vaughan, ed., *Early American Indian Documents: Treaties and Laws, 1607–1789* (Washington, DC: University Publications of America, 1979), 183–85. A good overall source on La Demoiselle/Old Briton is R. David Edmunds, "Old Briton," in *American Indian Leaders: Studies in Diversity*, ed. R. David Edmunds, 1–20 (Lincoln: University of Nebraska Press, 1980).

15. John D. Barnhart and Dorothy L. Riker, *Indiana to 1816: The Colonial Period*, vol. 1, The History of Indiana (Indianapolis: Indiana Historical Bureau and Indiana Historical Society, 1971), 142–45.

16. Gregory Evans Dowd, *A Spirited Resistance: The North American Indian Struggle for Unity, 1745–1815* (Baltimore, MD: Johns Hopkins University Press, 1992), explores at length the militant nativistic movements found through this period and later. Anthony F. C. Wallace, "New Religions among the Delaware Indians, 1600–1900," in *The Emergent Native Americans: A Reader in Culture Contact*, ed. Deward E. Walker, 344–61 (Boston: Little, Brown, 1971), explores the evolution of Christianity and the nativistic movement among the Delaware.

17. Barnhart and Riker, *Indiana to 1816*, 164–65.

18. Vergil E. Noble, "Ouiatenon on the Oubache: Archaeological Investigation at a Fur Trading Post on the Wabash River," in *French Colonial Archaeology* (see note 4), 66–77.

19. Neal Trubowitz, "Native Americans and French on the Central Wabash," in *Calumet & Fleur-de-lys: Archaeology of Indian and French Contact in the Midcontinent*, ed. John A. Walthall and Thomas E. Emerson, 241–64 (Washington, DC: Smithsonian Institution Press, 1992); James R. Jones, "Degrees of Acculturation at Two 18th Century Aboriginal Villages near Lafayette, Tippecanoe County, Indiana: Ethnohistoric and Archaeological Perspectives" (PhD diss., Indiana University, 1988).

CHAPTER 3:
Early American Period, 1783–1812

1. Peter Nabokov, *Native American Testimony: A Chronicle of Indian-White Relations from Prophecy to the Present, 1492–1992* (New York: Viking, 1991), 96–97.

2. A standard, holistic work is R. Carlyle Buley, *The Old Northwest: Pioneer Period, 1815–1840* (Indianapolis: Indiana Historical Society, 1950). Specific topics relating to this region are covered in Andrew R. L. Cayton, ed., *Pathways to the Old Northwest: An Observance of the Bicentennial of the Northwest Ordinance* (Indianapolis: Indiana Historical Society, 1988).

3. A recent biography of Little Turtle is Harvey Lewis Carter, *The Life and Times of Little Turtle: First Sagamore of the Wabash* (Urbana: University of Illinois Press, 1987).

4. A useful concept is discussed by Jacqueline Peterson in "Many Roads to Red River: Métis Genesis in the Great Lakes Region, 1680–1815," in *The New Peoples: Being and Becoming Métis in North America*, ed. Jacqueline Peterson and Jennifer S. H. Brown, 60 (Lincoln: University of Nebraska Press, 1985). Peterson defines "jack-knife" posts as "subsidiary trading outlets run by a single trader and his employees or by one or more trading families related by *blood or marriage*." Settlement at South Bend and Peru started as jack-knife posts.

5. Michael D. Green, "The Expansion of European Colonization to the Mississippi Valley, 1780–1880," in *North America*, vol. 1, part 1, ed. Bruce G. Trigger and Wilcomb E. Washburn, *The Cambridge History of the Native Peoples of the Americas*, 475–81 (New York: Cambridge University Press, 1996), gives an overall view of the situation leading to the Grand Councils. Wiley Sword, *President Washington's Indian War: The Struggle for the Old Northwest, 1790–1795* (Norman: University of Oklahoma Press, 1985), 20–21, describes this council briefly.

6. Charles J. Kappler, comp. and ed., *Indian Treaties, 1778–1883* (New York: Interland Publishing, 1972). Kappler has organized all U.S. Indian treaties in chronological order, indexed by tribe. These three early treaties that project U.S. attitude throughout the treaty process are discussed on pages 6–8 (1785), 16–17 (1786), and 18–23 (1789).

7. Sword, *President Washington's Indian War*, is a recent intensive analysis of this period.

8. Ibid., 101–30.

9. Ibid., 155–91.

10. In addition to Green, "The Expansion of European Colonization to the Mississippi Valley," in *North America* (see note 4), 480–81, and chapter 22 of Sword, *President Washington's Indian War*, a vivid description of this council is given in Isabel Thompson Kelsay, *Joseph Brant, 1743–1807: Man of Two Worlds* (Syracuse, NY: Syracuse University Press, 1984), 477–81.

11. Chapter 5 of Colin G. Calloway's recent work on the Shawnee, *The Shawnees and the War for America* (New York: Viking, 2007), gives some background on Blue Jacket and a somewhat Shawnee-centric view of the times.

12. Sword, *President Washington's Indian War*, 301–2.

13. Ibid., 258–311.

14. Wilbur M. Cunningham, ed., *Letter Book of William Burnett: Early Fur Trader in the Land of Four Flags* (St. Joseph, MI: Fort Miami Heritage Society of Michigan, 1967). William Burnett's trade record manuscripts are available on microfilm in the collection Northern Indiana Historical Society Local History Manuscripts, 1801–1970, University of Notre Dame Archives, Notre Dame, IN.

15. Charles N. Thompson, *Sons of the Wilderness: John and William Conner* (Indianapolis: Indiana Historical Society, 1937); John Lauritz Larson and David Vanderstel, "Agent of Empire: William Conner on the Indiana Frontier, 1800–1855," *Indiana Magazine of History* 80, no. 4 (December 1984): 301–28. Conner Prairie Interactive History Park in Fishers, Indiana, is an additional valuable source of information.

16. Ora Brooks Peake, *A History of the United States Indian Factory System, 1795–1822* (Denver: Sage Books, 1954), gives an overall history of the enterprise. Bert J. Griswold, ed., *Fort Wayne, Gateway of the West, 1802–1813: Garrison Orderly Books, Indian Agency Account Book* (Indianapolis: Indiana Historical Bureau, 1927), presents some of the factory accounts.

17. Logan Esarey, ed., *Messages and Letters of William Henry Harrison* (Indianapolis: Indiana Historical Commission, 1922), 1:240–43, 433–36, 437, 439; 2:50–59.

18. There are a number of biographies of Tecumseh; two recent ones are R. David Edmunds, *Tecumseh and the Quest for Indian Leadership*, 2d ed. (NY: Pearson Longman, 2007), and John Sugden, *Tecumseh: A Life* (New York: Henry Holt and Co., 1998).

19. Esarey, ed., *Messages and Letters of William Henry Harrison*, 1:457.

20. A recent biography of Tecumseh's brother is R. David Edmunds, *The Shawnee Prophet* (Lincoln: University of Nebraska Press, 1983). A further discussion of the Shawnee Prophet and Tecumseh can be found in chapter 7 of Gregory Evans Dowd, *A Spirited Resistance: The North American Indian Struggle for Unity, 1745–1815* (Baltimore, MD: Johns Hopkins University Press, 1992).

21. Paul Woehrmann, *At the Headwaters of the Maumee: A History of the Forts at Fort Wayne* (Indianapolis: Indiana Historical Society, 1971), 119–27, 136–41. The history of the Moravian mission is in Lawrence Henry Gipson, ed., *The Moravian Indian Mission on White River: Diaries and Letters, May 5, 1799, to November 12, 1806* (Indianapolis: Indiana Historical Bureau, 1938).

22. Helen Hornbeck Tanner and Miklos Pinther, *Atlas of Great Lakes Indian History*, vol. 174, The Civilization of the American Indian (Norman: Published for the Newberry Library by the University of Oklahoma Press, 1987), 106–11, provides a convenient listing and location map of the War of 1812 battles in the West. The Mississinewa confrontations are discussed in Elizabeth J. Glenn, "The Ethnohistory of the Battle of Mississinewa" in "Ethnohistorical and Archaeological Descriptive Accounts of the War of 1812: Mississinewa Campaign and Aftermath, Project Report," Elizabeth J. Glenn, B. K. Swartz, and Russell E. Lewis, 1–285 (Muncie, IN: Archaeological Reports of Ball State University, 1977).

CHAPTER 4:
Statehood to Indian Removal, 1812–1840

1. Bourassa's quote comes from John Tipton, *The John Tipton Papers*, comp. Glen A. Blackburn, and ed. Nellie A. Robertson and Dorothy L. Riker, vol. 2, *1828–1838* (Indianapolis: Indiana Historical Bureau, 1942), 645–46; Johnson's quote comes from Henderson Papers, H.497(10), Filson Club, Louisville, KY.

2. Logan Esarey, ed., *Messages and Letters of William Henry Harrison* (Indianapolis: Indiana Historical Commission, 1922), 1:71.

3. Gayle Thornbrough, ed., *Letter Book of the Indian Agency at Fort Wayne, 1809–1815* (Indianapolis: Indiana Historical Society, 1961), 252. The original manuscript is in the collection Fort Wayne Indian Agency Letterbooks, 1809–1815, in the William L. Clements Library, University of Michigan, Ann Arbor, MI.

4. Ibid.

5. Ibid., 253.

6. Robert A. Trennert, *Indian Traders on the Middle Border: The House of Ewing, 1827–54* (Lincoln: University of Nebraska Press, 1981).

7. Bert Anson, "The Early Years of Lathrop M. Taylor, The Fur Trader," *Indiana Magazine of History* 44 (December 1948): 367–83; Bert Anson, "Lathrop M. Taylor: Hanna and Taylor Partnership," *Indiana Magazine of History* 45 (June 1949): 147–70. The Northern Indiana Center for History Archives, South Bend, Indiana, holds Taylor's account books and ledgers, which give a good impression of the trade and provide individual accounts for particular Potawatomi shoppers. Anson's dissertation, "The Fur Traders in Northern Indiana, 1796–1850" (PhD diss., Indiana University, 1953), provides background and extensive lists of licensed traders of the era.

8. Paul Wallace Gates, "Introduction," in *John Tipton Papers*, 3 vols.

9. The texts of all American Indian treaties are found in chronological order in Charles J. Kappler, comp. and ed., *Indian Treaties, 1778–1883* (New York: Interland Publishing, 1972).

10. Joseph B. Herring, *Kenekuk, the Kickapoo Prophet* (Lawrence: University Press of Kansas, 1988).

11. Published primary accounts of the Potawatomi removal provide excellent examples of how this policy was effected. Examples include Irving McKee, ed., *The Trail of Death: Letters of Benjamin Marie Petit* (Indianapolis: Indiana Historical Society, 1941); Dwight Smith, "The Attempted Potawatomi Emigration of 1839," *Indiana Magazine of History* 45 (March 1949): 51–80; Dwight Smith, "A Continuation of the Journal of an Emigrating Party of Potawatomi Indians, 1838, and Ten William Polke Manuscripts," *Indiana Magazine of History* 44 (December 1948): 392–408; and Dwight Smith, "Jacob Hull's Detachment of the Potawatomi Emigration of 1838," *Indiana Magazine of History* 45 (September 1949): 285–88.

12. Shelley D. Rouse, "Colonel Dick Johnson's Choctaw Academy: A Forgotten Educational Experiment," *Ohio Archaeological and Historical Quarterly* 25, no. 1 (January 1916): 88–117.

13. Leland Winfield Meyer, *The Life and Times of Colonel Richard M. Johnson of Kentucky* (New York: Columbia University Press, 1932). A greater emphasis on Johnson's school is by Carolyn T. Foreman, "The Choctaw Academy," *Chronicles of Oklahoma* 6 (1928): 453–80, 9 (1931): 382–411, and 10 (1932): 77–114. Original papers from Choctaw Academy are available in the collection Richard M. Johnson: Miscellaneous Papers, 1814–1848, in the Filson Historical Society Library, Louisville, KY.

14. Isaac McCoy, *History of Baptist Indian Missions: Embracing Remarks on the Former and Present Conditions of the Aboriginal Tribes* (Washington, [DC?]: W. M. Morrison, 1840).

15. Foreman, "The Choctaw Academy," lists the students by tribe, and Kappler, *Indian Treaties*, 277, lists Carey Mission students, past and present, who received land grants. The approximate count comes from those two sources.

16. Timothy S. Smith, *Missionary Abomination Unmasked: Or, A View of Carey Mission Containing an Unmasking of the Missionary Abominations Practiced Among the Indians of St. Joseph County at the Celebrated Missionary Establishment Known as Carey Mission Under the Supervision of the Rev. Isaac McCoy* (South Bend, IN: The Beacon Office, 1833).

17. *John Tipton Papers*, vol. 3, *1834–1839*, 602–3.

18. *John Tipton Papers*, vol. 1, *1800–1827*, facing 408.

19. Charles C. Trowbridge and Vernon Kinietz, eds., *Meearmeear Traditions* (Ann Arbor: University of Michigan Press, 1938); Charles C. Trowbridge, Vernon Kinietz, and Erminie Wheeler-Voegelin, *Shawnese Traditions: C. C. Trowbridge's Account* (Ann Arbor: University of Michigan Press, 1939); George Winter, *The Journals and Indian Paintings of George Winter, 1837–1839* (Indianapolis: Indiana Historical Society, 1948); Sarah E. Cooke and Rachel Ramadhyani, comps., *Indians and a Changing Frontier: The Art of George Winter* (Indianapolis: Indiana Historical Society, in cooperation with the Tippecanoe County Historical Association, 1993).

CHAPTER 5:
After Indian Removal, 1840–1870

1. Records of the Washington Superintendency, Bureau of Indian Affairs, No. 75.15.14, RG 75, National Archives, available in the History Collection, University of Wisconsin Digital Collections, http://digicoll.library.wisc.edu/cgi-bin/History/History-dx?id=History.IT1854no274.

2. Andrew Bell-Fialkoff, "A Brief History of Ethnic Cleansing," *Foreign Affairs* (Summer 1993): 110–11, 113.

3. James A. Clifton, *The Pokagons, 1683–1983: Catholic Potawatomi Indians of the St. Joseph River Valley* (Lanham, MD: University Press of America, 1984), 47.

4. Ibid., 69, 71.

5. Ibid., 71–72.

6. Ibid., 82, 84.

7. Ibid., 85.

8. Ibid., 86–87.

9. Ibid., 88–89.

10. Bert Anson, *The Miami Indians*, The Civilization of the American Indian Series, vol. 103 (Norman: University of Oklahoma Press, 1970), 224–26; Stewart Rafert, *The Miami Indians of Indiana: A Persistent People, 1654–1994* (Indianapolis: Indiana Historical Society, 1996), 122.

11. Rafert, *Miami Indians of Indiana*, 123.

12. Ibid., 124.

13. Anson, *Miami Indians*, 236; Rafert, *Miami Indians of Indiana*, 124.

14. Rafert, *Miami Indians of Indiana*, 118.

15. George Winter, *The Journals and Indian Paintings of George Winter, 1837–1839* (Indianapolis: Indiana Historical Society, 1948), 160–62.

16. Miami County, IN, Auditor's Office, Deed Book V, 530; Stewart J. Rafert, "The Hidden Community: The Miami Indians of Indiana, 1846–1940" (PhD diss., University of Delaware, 1982), 173.

17. Rafert, "The Hidden Community," 173.

18. Rafert, *Miami Indians of Indiana*, 136.

19. "Testimony Pursuant to Congressional Legislation of June 1, 1872," ISP Shelf 8, Entry 310, 410–11, RG 75, National Archives.

20. Sarah Wadsworth interview, October 10, 1909, Jacob P. Dunn Papers, Notebook 1, Indiana State Library, Indianapolis.

21. Rafert, *Miami Indians of Indiana*, 132, 142–43.

22. Rafert, "The Hidden Community," 115–16.

23. Anson, *Miami Indians*, 269–70.

24. Rafert, *Miami Indians of Indiana*, 125–26.

25. Ibid., 126–27.

26. Rafert, *Miami Indians of Indiana*, 127; Anson, *Miami Indians*, 272.

27. House Executive Document 23, 49th Cong., 1st Sess., vol. 25, Jan. 4, 1886, Serial 2392 discusses the negotiations. The treaty is printed in Charles J. Kappler, ed., *Indian Affairs: Laws and Treaties*, 2d ed., vol. 2 (Washington, DC: Government Printing Office, 1904), 644.

28. Council Book, Miami Nation of Indians, 1937–42, Miami Nation Tribal Archives, Peru, Indiana.

29. Rafert, *Miami Indians of Indiana*, 129.

30. Ibid., 130.

31. Ibid.

CHAPTER 6:
Tribalism Endangered, 1870–1900

1. Lawrence W. Schultz, "Godfroy Family Genealogy," Miami County Historical Society, Peru, Indiana.

2. James A. Clifton, *The Pokagons, 1683–1983: Catholic Potawatomi Indians of the St. Joseph River Valley* (Lanham, MD: University Press of America, 1984), 94.

3. Ibid., 91.

4. Ibid., 90.

5. Ibid., 92, 94.

6. Ibid., 95–96.

7. Ibid., 96, 100.

8. Ibid., 101.

9. Ibid., 102.

10. Ibid., 105.

11. Ibid., 106; Pam-to-Pee v. U.S., 187 U.S. 371 (1902).

12. Stewart Rafert, *The Miami Indians of Indiana: A Persistent People, 1654–1994* (Indianapolis: Indiana Historical Society, 1996), 139.

13. *An Act to Authorize the Secretary of the Interior to Make Partition of the Reservation to Me-shin-go-me-sia, a Miami Indian*, in Statutes at Large of the United States of America, 1789–1873, 42d Cong., 2d Sess., vol. 17, June 1, 1872, 213–14.

14. *Book Relating to Land Disposition of Me-shin-go-me-sia Reservation* in Records of the Bureau of Indian Affairs, 1800–1895, RG 75, National Archives; microfilm copy available in the William Henry Smith Memorial Library, Indiana Historical Society, Indianapolis.

15. Surveyors' Field Notes, ISP Shelf 8, Entry 310, RG 75, National Archives; Plat Map No. 1: "Preliminary Survey," and Plat Map. No. 2: "Extent in Acres of Each Allotment," Central Map Files #120, RG 75, National Archives.

16. *Act to Authorize the Secretary of the Interior to Make Partition of the Reservation to Me-shin-go-me-sia*, 213–14.

17. The loss of Bundy's property is culled from the following Wabash County, Indiana, records: Clerk's Office, guardianship box 88, packet 20; Recorder's Office, Deed Record 41, p. 117; Mortgage Record 4, p. 405; and Chattel Record, p. 193. For an overview, see Rafert, *Miami Indians of Indiana*, 154–55.

18. Rafert, *Miami Indians of Indiana*, 157–58. Jacob Piatt Dunn took Peconga's description of his farm in the Miami language. Dunn's translation is in the Jacob P. Dunn Papers, Indiana State Library, Indianapolis.

19. Rafert, *Miami Indians of Indiana*, 164–66. See map, page 167, for Miami sites in Miami County.

20. *Wau-pe-man-qua*, alias *Mary Strack, v. Aldrich*, 28 F. 489, 494 (1886).

21. *Board of Commissioners of Allen County v. Simons, Trustee, et al.*, 28 N.E. 420 (1891); *Acts of Indiana*, Indiana General Assembly, 57th regular sess., 1891, 115; Bert Anson, *The Miami Indians*, The Civilization of the American Indian series, vol. 103 (Norman: University of Oklahoma Press, 1970), 279–80.

22. Anson, *Miami Indians*, 279; Rafert, *Miami Indians of Indiana*, 166.

23. Anson, *Miami Indians*, 253. See Rafert, *Miami Indians of Indiana*, 168–70, for the interesting history of this Indiana Miami colony in Indian Territory. The Indiana Miami in the West were listed as "Miami Indians of Indiana now living in Kansas, Quapaw Agency, Indian Territory, and Oklahoma Territory."

24. Rafert, *Miami Indians of Indiana*, 170–72.

25. Peter Iverson, *Carlos Montezuma and the Changing World of American Indians* (Albuquerque: University of New Mexico Press, 1982), 33–34; Zitkala-Ša, *American Indian Stories* (Lincoln: University of Nebraska Press, 1985), xii–xiii.

26. Rafert, *Miami Indians of Indiana*, 172–73; Office of Indian Affairs, Correspondence, Land Division, vol. 176, 412–13, RG 75, National Archives.

27. Rafert, *Miami Indians of Indiana*, 172–73. Van Devanter's full opinion is in *Decisions Relating to the Public Lands*, vol. 25 (Washington, DC: Government Printing Office, 1881–1921), 426–32.

28. Rafert, *Miami Indians of Indiana*, 175. *Board of Commissioners of Miami County v. Godfroy*, 60 N.E. 177–80 (1901) is the entire decision.

29. Rafert, *Miami Indians of Indiana*, 176; Office of Indian Affairs, LR 4378, January 22, 1898, RG 75, National Archives.

30. Rafert, *Miami Indians of Indiana*, 176; Office of Indian Affairs, LS 46376, November 23, 1901, RG 75, National Archives.

31. Rafert, *Miami Indians of Indiana*, 166, table 6:1.

CHAPTER 7:

Preserving Indian Ethnicity and Tribal Identity, 1900–1945

1. Hazel Hertzberg, *The Search for an American Indian Identity: Modern Pan-Indian Movements* (Syracuse, NY: Syracuse University Press, 1971), 300, 302.

2. Stewart Rafert, *The Miami Indians of Indiana: A Persistent People, 1654–1994* (Indianapolis: Indiana Historical Society, 1996), 199, 201.

3. Rafert, *Miami Indians of Indiana*, 189–90; "Miami Tribe Will Open 'Pow-wow' in Reunion of Members Here Today," *Huntington Press*, August 30, 1925; "Miami Descendants Gather for Annual Powwow Here," *Huntington Press*, September 1, 1925.

4. Swan Hunter and Eva Bossley, interview with Stewart Rafert, 1978; George S. Cottman, "Gleaned from the Pioneers," *Indiana Magazine of History* 1 (March 1905): 19–21.

5. Gabriel Godfroy, speech at Tippecanoe Battlefield Site, June 16, 1907, from Lawrence W. Schultz, "Godfroy Family Genealogy," Miami County Historical Society, Peru, Indiana.

6. Rafert, *Miami Indians of Indiana*, 187.

7. Rafert, *Miami Indians of Indiana*, 193–94; David J. Costa, *The Miami-Illinois Language* (Lincoln: University of Nebraska Press, 2003), 23–25.

8. Rafert, *Miami Indians of Indiana*, 210–11.

9. Stewart Rafert, "Individual Survey Form, Gabriel Tucker," from Rafert research notes on Miami Indians.

10. U.S. Bureau of the Census, Twelfth Census of the United States, 1900, for Butler Township, Miami County, Indiana; U.S. Bureau of the Census, Thirteenth Census of the United States, 1910, Butler Township, Miami County, Indiana; U.S. Bureau of the Census, "Table 10: Indian Population of the Different States by Tribes, 1910," in *Indian Population in the United States and Alaska, 1910*, 22 (Washington, DC: Government Printing Office, 1915), available online at http://www.census.gov/.

11. James S. Olson and Raymond Wilson, *Native Americans in the Twentieth Century* (Urbana: University of Illinois Press, 1986), 96–101.

12. Rafert, *Miami Indians of Indiana*, 205–7. In the 1920s Bundy told Milford Chandler, a museum collector, the story of a Miami war pipe he was selling, which included references to these powers. See David Penney, *Art of the American Indian Frontier* (Seattle: University of Washington Press, 1992), 295–98.

13. The items and other Miami heirlooms are pictured in Penney, *Art of the American Indian Frontier*, 295–98.

14. Charles Burke to Camillus Bundy, June 20, 1927, Office of Indian Affairs, LS 28876, RG 75, National Archives, quoted in Rafert, *Miami Indians of Indiana*, 208.

15. Rafert, *Miami Indians of Indiana*, 209; "Unknown to Dr. Marschalk, May 22, 1929," 38901-1923-General Service File 302, RG 75, National Archives.

16. Rafert, *Miami Indians of Indiana*, 212.

17. "Death of Miami Chief's Daughter Ends Fight of Tribe for Large Area of State," *Indianapolis Star*, February 17, 1930.

18. Rafert, *Miami Indians of Indiana*, 214–16.

19. Rafert, *Miami Indians of Indiana*, 217; Glenn Griswold to Bureau of Indian Affairs, February 11, 1932, Office of Indian Affairs, LR 7791, file 1492-1910-Seneca-013, RG 75, National Archives.

20. Rafert, *Miami Indians of Indiana*, 217; Elijah Shapp to Harold L. Ickes, September 12, 1933, and July 1, 1933, Office of Indian Affairs, LR 7791, file 1492-1910-Seneca-013, RG 75, National Archives.

21. Olson and Wilson, *Native Americans in the Twentieth Century*, 100.

22. Willard W. Cochrane, *The Development of American Agriculture: A Historical Analysis* (Minneapolis: University of Minnesota Press, 1979), 100–101, 112–13, 116–21, 140–43; M. Teresa Baer, "From Tribal and Family Farmers to Part-time and Corporate Farmers: Two Hundred Years of Indiana Agriculture," in *Centennial Farms of Indiana*, ed. M. Teresa Baer, Kathleen M. Breen, Judith Q. McMullen, 15–40 (Indianapolis: Indiana Historical Society Press, 2003).

23. Olson and Wilson, *Native Americans in the Twentieth Century*, 109–15, gives an overview of the Indian New Deal and the reversal of older assimilationist policies.

24. Rafert, *Miami Indians of Indiana*, 223–24. This section is based on the many documents in Indian Reorganization File for the Indiana Miami, 1492-1910-Seneca-013, RG 75, National Archives.

25. Rafert, *Miami Indians of Indiana*, 224; D'Arcy McNickle, Memorandum to Tribal Organization Branch, Bureau of Indian Affairs, January 14, 1938, and William Zimmerman Jr. to Evans and DeWitt, February 1, 1938, 1492-1910-Seneca-013, RG 75, National Archives.

26. Rafert, *Miami Indians of Indiana*, 227.

27. Mildred Bundy to President Franklin D. Roosevelt, June 7, 1933, 38901-1923-General Service-File 302, RG 75, National Archives.

28. Rafert, *Miami Indians of Indiana*, 228.

29. James A. Clifton, *The Pokagons, 1683–1983: Catholic Potawatomi Indians of the St. Joseph River Valley* (Lanham, MD: University Press of America, 1984), 116.

30. Ibid., 117.

31. Ibid., 118.

32. Ibid., 119.

33. Ibid., 120.

34. Michael Yellowbird and C. Matthew Snipp, "American Indian Families," in *Minority Families in the United States: A Multicultural Perspective*, 3d ed., ed. Ronald L. Taylor, chapter 12 (Upper Saddle River, NJ: Prentice Hall, 2002).

35. Clifton, *Pokagons*, 121–23.

CHAPTER 8:
The Rise of Modern Tribalism and American Indian Ethnicity, 1945–2008

1. Records of the Indian Claims Commission, 1946–1983, RG 279, National Archives.

2. James S. Olson and Raymond Wilson, *Native Americans in the Twentieth Century* (Urbana: University of Illinois Press, 1986), 131–33, 135.

3. Stewart Rafert, *The Miami Indians of Indiana: A Persistent People, 1654–1994* (Indianapolis: Indiana Historical Society, 1996), 237–39; James A. Clifton, *The Pokagons, 1683–1983: Catholic Potawatomi Indians of the St. Joseph River Valley* (Lanham, MD: University Press of America, 1984), 130.

4. Rafert, *Miami Indians of Indiana*, 240, 257–58.

5. Troy R. Johnson, Joane Nagel, and Duane Champagne, *American Indian Activism: Alcatraz to the Longest Walk* (Urbana: University of Illinois Press, 1997), 53.

6. Joane Nagel, *American Indian Ethnic Renewal: Red Power and the Resurgence of Identity and Culture* (New York: Oxford University Press, 1997), 126–30, 158.

7. Ibid., 167.

8. Wilma Mankiller, *Mankiller: A Chief and Her People* (New York: St. Martin's Press, 1993), 192–93.

9. Nagel, *American Indian Ethnic Renewal*, 85.

10. Ibid.

11. Campbell Gibson and Kay Jung, "Table 29: Indiana—Race and Hispanic Origin, 1800 to 1990," in "Historical Census Statistics on Population Totals by Race, 1790 to 1990, and by Hispanic Origin, 1970 to 1990, for the United States, Regions, Divisions, and States," Working Paper Series No. 56 (Washington, DC: U.S. Bureau of the Census, 2002), available online at http://www.census.gov/; Stella U. Ogunwole, "Table 2: American Indian and Alaska Native Population for the United States, Regions, and States, and for Puerto Rico, 1990 and 2000, in "The American Indian and Alaska Native Population, 2000," 5 (Washington, DC: U.S. Bureau of the Census, 2002), available online at http://www.census.gov/.

12. Nagel, *American Indian Ethnic Renewal*, 91.

13. Ibid., 92–93.

14. Ibid., 91–92.

15. Sherman Goldenberg, "Indians Take Aim at State Schools' Archaeologists," *Fort Wayne Journal Gazette*, April 15, 1981.

16. Sherman Goldenberg, "Indiana Tribes Take Stand Against AIM," *Fort Wayne Journal Gazette*, July 18, 1981.

17. Ibid.

18. Elizabeth Glenn, personal communication to Stewart Rafert, August 5, 2008.

19. Rafert, *Miami Indians of Indiana*, 280–81.

20. Roger L. Nichols, *American Indians in U.S. History* (Norman: University of Oklahoma Press, 2003), 225.

21. Alvin M. Josephy Jr., *Red Power: The American Indians' Fight for Freedom* (Lincoln: University of Nebraska Press, 1985), 213.

22. William T. Hagan, *American Indians*, 3d ed. (Chicago: University of Chicago Press, 1993), 210.

23. Rafert, *Miami Indians of Indiana*, 268–69.

24. Ibid., 279.

25. Clifton, *Pokagons*, 131.

26. Rafert, *Miami Indians of Indiana*, 283; Eddie Brown, Assistant Secretary of Interior, Indian Affairs, to Raymond O. White, July 12, 1990, Miami Nation Tribal Archives, Peru, Indiana.

27. Rafert, *Miami Indians of Indiana*, 284; Branch of Acknowledgment and Research, Bureau of Indian Affairs, "Summary Under the Criteria and Evidence for Proposed Finding Against Federal Acknowledgment of the Miami Nation of Indians of the State of Indiana, Inc.," 11, available online at http://www.doi.gov/bia/.

28. Mark Edwin Miller, *Forgotten Tribes: Unrecognized Indians and the Federal Acknowledgment Process* (Lincoln: University of Nebraska Press, 2004), 53.

29. Rafert, *Miami Indians of Indiana*, 288–95; *Miami Nation of Indians of the State of Indiana, Inc., et. al. v. U.S. Department of the Interior, et. al.*, 255 F.3d 342 (2001). Full text of decision available online at http://www.findlaw.com/casecode/.

30. Native American Constitution and Law Digitization Project, "U.S. Supreme Court Update 2001–2002 Term," available online at http://madison.law.ou.edu/.

31. Pokagon Band of Potawatomi Indians official Web site, http://www.pokagon.com/.

CONCLUSION

1. Rebecca Martin, e-mail message to Stewart Rafert, August 15, 2008.

2. Stella U. Ogunwole, "Table 2: American Indian and Alaska Native Population for the United States, Regions, and States, and for Puerto Rico, 1990 and 2000, in "The American Indian and Alaska Native Population, 2000," 5 (Washington, DC: U.S. Bureau of the Census, 2002), available online at http://www.census.gov/.

3. U.S. Bureau of the Census, "Table 29: American Indian and Alaska Native Alone and Alone or in Combination Population by Tribe for Indiana, 2000," in "American Indian and Alaska Native Tribes for the United States, Regions, Divisions, and States (PHC-T-18) (Washington, DC: U.S. Bureau of the Census, 2002; rev. 2004), available online at http://www.census.gov/; U.S. Bureau of the Census, American FactFinder, Census 2000 Summary File 1, http://factfinder.census.gov/.

4. Joane Nagel, *American Indian Ethnic Renewal: Red Power and the Resurgence of Identity and Culture* (New York: Oxford University Press, 1997), 235.

5. Rita T. Kohn and Stands Tall Woman, "The Woodland People," *Indiana Historian* (September 2001): 13.

6. Joan Weibel-Orlando, *Indian Country, L.A.: Maintaining Ethnic Community in Complex Society* (Urbana: University of Illinois Press, 1991), 34, 38–39.

7. Ibid., 197.

8. Miami Nation of Indiana official Web site, http://www.miamiindians.org/.

9. Scott Shoemaker, e-mail message to Stewart Rafert, July 9, 2008.

10. The Pokagon Band of Potawatomi official Web site, http://www.pokagon.com/.

11. Lauren Viera, "Casino Brings a Crowd to Harbor Country," *Chicago Tribune*, November 25, 2007, available online at http://www.chicagotribune.com/.

Index

Page numbers in boldface indicate illustrations and maps.

c